MEMOIRS

OF

PERCY WALKER

Produced by
Blaisdon Publishing
3 Park Chase, Hornby, Bedale
North Yorkshire DL8 1PR
www.blaisdon.force9.co.uk

Reprinted 2004, 2005, 2007

Binding by *Remploy Ltd*

ISBN 978 190283818 2
(1 90283818 1)

Cover design: Bruce Webb

To Aileen and My Family

I have recorded the recollections of an ordinary
person living through a period of extraordinary
change.

Many things have changed for the better

but people of goodwill throughout the world face an
enormous challenge to prevent disasters in the
future.

A .P. Walker 2002

Contents

List of Illustrations

The Wedding Reception of my Mother and Father – Marine Hotel, Troon, 20th June

The Wedding of my Father and Mother

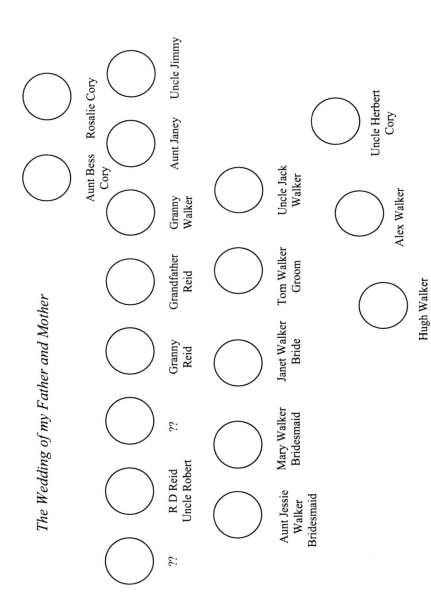

?? R D Reid Granny Grandfather Granny Aunt Bess Rosalie Cory
Uncle Robert Reid Reid Walker Cory

Aunt Jessie Mary Walker Janet Walker Tom Walker Uncle Jack Aunt Janey Uncle Jimmy
Walker Bridesmaid Bride Groom Walker
Bridesmaid

Hugh Walker Alex Walker Uncle Herbert
Cory

15

Early Years at Campbellfield

I was born on 2nd July 1916 at Campbellfield, Kilwinning Road, Irvine, Ayrshire – my parents being Thomas Campbell Walker and Janet Gilmour Reid or Walker. Both Walkers and Reids were old local families for generations. The battle of the Somme was raging at the time of my birth. In those days, the Family Doctor delivered all babies at home and in the main, these doctors possessed skills for difficult cases, mainly because the 'buck stopped with them'. By and large, they were good at their job – they had to be!

Campbellfield was a lovely old typically Scottish detached house; six bedrooms (not including separate quarters, en suite, for cook and housemaid). 'Nanny' slept in the night nursery with the currently youngest child. My sister Kathleen preceded me by 2½ years being born on 24th March 1914.

Percy in the arms of Nurse McCrae ~ July 1916

Campbellfield, Irvine

My Grandfather and Grandmother Reid, with their daughter, Winnie my Aunt, with cousins, Willie and Mary Breckenridge, and my sister, Kathleen and myself ~ 1918

Kilwinning Road, Irvine, in those days contained the houses of my paternal grandmother and her unmarried daughter, my maternal grandfather and grandmother, four uncles and aunts and, in due course, many cousins.

I was just old enough to remember Armistice Day on 11 November 1918. What slaughter! What for? What bravery and endurance!

Kathleen and Percy ~ Armistice Day 1918

Our family connection was luckier than most in that the family breadwinners returned home relatively unscathed after the horrors of the Great War. How must they have felt when their sons and daughters were called upon to serve their country in war 21 years later!

My recollections of childhood are that of an idyllic life. We had a lovely house and garden. We were not wealthy, but never lacked for anything. My father took a delight in his garden, keeping it in perfect condition, although nearly all the work was done by the wonderful Tom McLean, our full-time gardener for many years. Annie Murphy, our cook from Dundalk in Ireland regularly produced 'Five Star' meals and Jean McGinn, our housemaid, like Annie were real friends of the family.

My mother telephoned the local shops daily, after which the message boys would cycle to Campbellfield with everything we needed.

My Mother and Father
Janet Gilmour Reid Walker   *Thomas Campbell Walker*

My mother was a very gentle soul. She lived for her family and home and was not greatly interested in events beyond her own circle. She was a very talented artist and excellent with any form of handiwork, and we have many lovely reminders of her skill.

Motorcars in those days were thin on the ground. I remember going to Glasgow in my Granny Walker's Buick, with Kathleen and my mother, on a shopping expedition. Granny Walker's chauffeur, King, was under orders to pull up to a stop if he encountered another car on the road.

Another trip to Glasgow was a great treat for me. Leaving Irvine Bank Street Station on the Caledonian Railway Train 1st Class, change at Kilwinning East and proceed to Glasgow Central. This line for the Arran Boat Train to Ardrôssan Montgomerie Pier became redundant in the 50's and now terminates at Neilston, near Glasgow. It never really competed with the Glasgow and South Western Railway from St. Enoch's to Ardrossan, Ayr and beyond.

Robert arrived on 9th November 1920. Kathleen and I had had the formidable Nurse McCrae as Monthly Nurse, but Robert had Nurse Knox. I recall seeing the newly arrived infant having a bath in front of the fire. He let fly with a stream into the fire, which fascinated me so much, that I said, "Do that again Nurse," to which she replied, "My boy that is something I cannot do".

Kathleen and I would accompany Nanny and the baby in the pram almost every day on a walk round the town or to the shore. We also had a pony, Bessie, and a trap in which, with Nanny holding the reins, we would trot miles around the countryside.

My mother would spend her days knitting, sewing and keeping the house perfect and telephoning her sister Winnie, two houses away. She and her children visited our grandparents almost every day. My father went to work in his office at Walker's Chemical Works, Irvine (later to be part of ICI at Ardeer). He was very 'hands on' and knew all of his workforce and their family circumstances. 'Big Tam' was really loved by his employees as an enlightened employer. He did a 'round' of 'The Works' every day and nothing escaped him. After everything was to his satisfaction and his letters signed, he had time for a game of golf almost every day (and was to inspire his sons to do likewise!)

After Robert arrived, Kathleen and our cousin Mary Breckenridge, next door but one, played together and were always life-long friends. Mary's brother Willie, 3 years older than I, was my hero. He was killed in Burma in 1942. He weaned me off playing with dolls. I recall, once with Willie's encouragement, decapitating my doll, Aileen, with the wheels of my tricycle. This was not prophetic, as I subsequently married an Aileen in 1946, and have lived with her blissfully happily ever after!

Our pony, Bessie, Nana, Kathleen and Percy in the trap

Robert and I had a 'playhouse' where we kept a state-of-the-art *Hornby* Railway. We graduated from clockwork to electric and eventually had a centralised control system of points and signals. I had control of the trains until Robert was considered to be capable of running them. His job until then was to transport passengers, freight and livestock by road to the railway towing cars, lorries and buses by a string. In the playhouse's heyday we ran all train services to a strict timetable, modelled on real life.

Between playhouse sessions we played tennis for hours on end on a lovely 'En tout cas' hard court. Willie Cunningham came up from the Works on his bicycle daily to brush and roll the court ready for play.

We also had an 18-hole putting green kept in immaculate condition. I wish that I could putt as well now! We thought we were doing badly if we failed to hole 10 footers! My father was a brilliant putter.

Swimming in Troon and Prestwick open-air pools or on the shore at Irvine, a beautiful unspoiled stretch of sand, were regular summer pastimes. The pools were unheated but we never noticed.

We holidayed every summer at Elie, Fife, a lovely East Coast resort. We had the same house for years on end. Elie was and still is, a wonderful place for holidays, for all ages. A normal day would start with golf, then tennis, at least one swim per day. A visit to 'The Peirots', amateur song and dance in the Earlsferry Town Hall and parties in friends' houses, all blissful and innocent!

Golf, my father's passion was always to the fore. Robert became and still is a very good golfer. He was, and still is a very good tennis player. Unlike me, he practiced sport whenever he could in spite of having a natural aptitude for games.

For our early education we all attended a Kindergarten School under the auspices of governesses, first Miss Dickson and later Miss Anderson. They were trained as teachers of the very young by The Parents National Educational Union. I wonder if it still exists? Lessons took place at our cousins, the Breckenridge's house. What we learned from these two ladies stood us all in good stead for our entry later to boarding school.

Education

At the age of 10 years I went to Cambusdoon Preparatory School in Alloway, Ayr. Life was good there. We were well taught and disciplined and well fed in the most beautiful surroundings on 'ye banks and braes o' bonny Doon'. I was a boarder there but we went home on Sunday afternoons after Church in Alloway Kirk beside the Auld Kirk where Tam o'Shanter saw the witches.

Cambusdoon, Alloway, Ayr ~ My Preparatory School

How sad that circumstances have changed and that this great school disappeared like so many other Preparatory Schools. Even worse, the beautiful stately home, in which the school was situated, was demolished and the lovely grounds are now full of desirable residences. After 4 years at Cambusdoon I went to Shrewsbury School, one of England's top Public Schools.

I think that there was then a feeling abroad amongst the relatively well to do in Scotland that their children's outlook on life should be less parochial and their horizons widened (and possibly their accents 'improved'?)

Shrewsbury School
The Boathouse on the River Severn and school buildings above

Shrewsbury School Officers' Training Corps
en route for Bellerby Camp, at Leyburn Station, Yorkshire ~ 1932

I owe a tremendous amount to Shrewsbury and my absorption of its traditions. Although life was tough there it did me no harm to be toughened up! At Shrewsbury, exercises and games were undertaken with fervour whether voluntarily or not. Cross-country runs were hellish but being pushed up to the limit of endurance was to stand me in good stead. We could do more with some of that nowadays.

Percy at Shrewsbury in 'Weekday Rig' – note Eton collar   *Percy at Shrewsbury in 'Sunday Rig'*

I sometimes regret not having gone to an equally good Scottish Public School, mainly because in later life one would be far more likely, living in Scotland, to work and play amongst old school friends. On balance, I am very glad to have been at Shrewsbury, and my only regret about my time there is that after my first two years enjoying and being fairly good at Arts and Language subjects, I was switched to the Science side. I have no aptitude whatever for Scientific subjects or for Mathematics, both of which delayed my succeeding in obtaining my School Certificate. However, I eventually managed to obtain my University Entrance Certificate. I owe a great deal to a Master at Shrewsbury who, realising that I was floundering with the Sciences, felt that my abilities might lead me to a career in Medicine. He was right! I found subjects such as biology and physiology totally fascinating and, in fact, I managed to get through all my examinations timeously at the University of Glasgow whence I qualified MBChB in 1939 – to the astonishment of my teachers at Shrewsbury when I turned up for Speech Day in June 1940 in my uniform as 'Temporary Acting Surgeon Lieutenant Royal Naval Volunteer Reserve'!

Entering Glasgow University in the autumn of 1934 was a totally different life! More of that later.

Music

$\mathcal{A}$ ll during my childhood and early teenage years, our house was filled with music all day (and often at night in bed with earphones). Sunday evenings were round the piano with our father strumming favourite children's hymns. Strangely, our local Catholic Priest, Father Murphy, was a regular visitor; I suspect that information about 'sure things' at the Races was exchanged. The Walkers and Reids were all Presbyterians, and long time members of Irvine Old Parish Church. The graveyard there contains many relations. There was a 'Reid' pew, a 'Walker' pew and a 'Breckenridge' pew. All these families walked to church from their homes every Sunday. I remember the Earl of Eglinton and his family on their way to the Parish Church passing our door in their carriage and four with footmen postillions. Eglinton Castle is now sadly no more, like so many great houses.

We had *H.M.V.* portable gramophones, which used thick needles for loudness; thin ones for less loud and wooden ones for almost imperceptibility.

The big bands were always popular. Jack Hylton, Jack Payne, Jack Jackson, Henry Hall, Roy Fox, Ambrose, Geraldo, Sydney Lipton, Carroll Gibbons and Harry Roy come to mind. I subliminally absorbed the music and lyrics of those days and still remember almost every word. The favourite music later would often be Fred Astaire and Ginger Rogers from their films. We had an extension loudspeaker down by the tennis court — our neighbours (the Murrays who were between us and our cousins the Breckenridges) were very tolerant.

It is still a pleasure to hear these wonderful bands recorded on the radio, as I cannot listen to modern beat repetitive noises. I often think that the music of these bygone days led to fantasies of pleasant things. Sadly, the pop music of today seems perhaps to have the opposite effect on today's young. Seventy years on I still find light classical music on radio, tape or CD my best tranquilliser, apart from whisky!

Apart from sporting activities, in our younger days our exercise was on tricycles towing 'bogies' which frequently terrorised our passengers.

No summer passed in both my prep school and public school days without a visit to Airds Bay, Loch Etive, home of my great friend Kenneth Macleod. From there we had our annual cruise in the Macleod yacht *Volva* to the Western Isles.

VOLVA

Cabin Cruiser belonging to Macleods of Taynuilt, in which I had my annual West Highland cruise in the 30's

University

$\mathcal{T}$o revert to my years at Glasgow University, I was very lucky, possibly due to the fact that many Professors of Glasgow University were members of Troon Golf Club and friends of my father, I was enrolled in the Medical Faculty in the autumn of 1934, a couple of months after leaving school. Many had to wait for at least a year.

University of Glasgow ~ Medical Student 1934-39

Our first year subjects, Physics and Chemistry cropped up again but, with a mixture of hard work and luck, I was able to convince the examiners that I was just good enough for pass marks. In our first year we also did Zoology and Botany. I wish now I remembered more about these subjects. Second year was

Anatomy and Physiology. This required an enormous amount of studying but I really enjoyed my attempts to be good at these subjects. This basic training by excellent teachers of worldwide fame greatly helped me in later practical medical studies. Third year was Pathology and Materia Medica (the latter now known as Pharmacology.)

Professor Shaw Dunn had written a famous textbook on Pathology but his lectures consisted of reading out loud several chapters of his book whilst the students feverishly wrote down his words of wisdom. When it came to actually learning for the examinations we read his book and not our almost illegible writings. I recall at the start of the lectures that old 'chronic' students used to shout out "attendance, attendance" before the lecturer was allowed to start. This ensured the acquisition of sufficient attendance marks to qualify for the Class Certificate, essential to avoid being kicked out. These 'chronics' were happy enough not to pass their exams because a rich aunt had vowed to endow them with whatever was necessary to keep body and soul together for the duration of their student life! A good friend of mine took over 10 years to qualify, his aunt having passed on!

Fourth year was Medical Jurisprudence and Public Health. They were very interesting subjects, well taught by experts in their field, again of international renown. I made the mistake of thinking that they were relatively easy subjects and spent more time enjoying myself in extra mural activities than I should. I was horrified not to pass first time but I really worked hard cooped up in my digs in Byres Road, Glasgow during a lovely summer, getting down to it for my resit. My examiner, second time round, said that my second attempt was as good as my first one had been bad!

Fifth year was Surgery, Medicine and Midwifery. We had had a little introduction to Midwifery in our fourth year. This consisted of crowding into a large operating theatre where the legendary Professor Sam Cameron would arrive at The Royal Maternity

Hospital, Rottenrow, after a good luncheon at his Club in his grey morning coat complete with carnation.

An emaciated little lady suffering from Rickets, so prevalent in those days because of poor nutrition and lack of milk and sunlight – the latter due to the persistent fog – was on the operating table, obviously very pregnant. Rachitic Dwarfs, as they were known, were given employment in the bowels of the hospitals because the passages underground were less than 5ft. high. After being anaesthetised by chloroform on a mask, Sam would then make a bold incision and pull out a perfect baby by the feet. The chronics would clap if he had beaten his previous record, time-wise, and 'boo' if he had not. Sam would say to his assistant, "Stitch her up please," and return from whence he came – his Club. Sam was, however, a wonderful obstetrician and teacher who did an enormous amount of work to make the Glasgow School famous and he also had a huge private practice.

In our Fifth Year we embarked on 'hands on' midwifery and were very well taught both in theory and practice. This stood me in good stead when, after the war, working in Ayrshire Central Maternity Hospital, Irvine, I took and obtained the Diploma of the Royal College of Obstetricians and Gynaecologists.

During our summer holidays lectures were suspended but we worked extremely hard attached to either medical or surgical units in the various hospitals in Glasgow. I was lucky enough to be accepted into Professor McNee's firm in the Western Infirmary where I learnt a huge amount and enjoyed it all. I did my surgery under Professor Burton at The Royal Infirmary, Glasgow, again a first class teaching unit.

In those days the patients whom we encountered were by and large not admitted to hospital with a great likelihood of being sent home cured.

A typical day in an operating theatre consisted of doing one's best for poor people – too poor to afford a doctor until almost terminal, and being admitted purely for palliative reasons. So we gained our knowledge not so much on early diagnosis but on well-advanced diseases and injuries. As well as attending our own medical surgical units by day, for a fortnight in our final year we had to do what was called 'District Midwifery'. We lived in a hostel beside Rottenrow Hospital and were called out, in rotation, between 6pm.and 6am. to ladies in labour in their own homes. A runner would rush .to the hospital and request immediate help for a poor woman in pangs of labour. No antenatal care in those days for the poor! Two of us would leap on to a tram car (the nicht caur as it was called) and proceed to a tenement – "Oh, thank God you're here, doctor, she's awfu' bad." This was really being put in at the deep end. The home circumstances demonstrated unbelievable poverty – a huge bed with half naked children beside the mother, who was having yet another baby. The husband, I recall in one case, coughing, no doubt tuberculosis sputum, into the basin (cold water tap only). The bedclothes were newspapers.

I was lucky in that nature helped me with almost all my cases, twenty of them. The only unlucky thing was when a pair of young nurses turned up at 5.55am and would claim the baby as theirs if we could not persuade Mum to push hard enough before six o'clock in the morning. It was difficult to stay awake during our daytime activities, but good practice for being a GP later! It was hard work doing all the practical work in these three main subjects and preparing for the final examinations simultaneously. There was no substitute for intense, dedicated studying. In my case, my perseverance was helped by the fact that our family fortunes, such as they were, suffered severely from the 1929 market crash, in which my father saw his fortune decimated almost overnight. He borrowed and borrowed to keep us all at schools and University (no subsidised fees in those days). I sometimes think that getting through my exams in the minimum time was, even if only subconsciously, due to these factors.

University Social Life/Sports

*H*owever, my social life at Glasgow University was wonderful to look back on. I made many friends, both inside the University and in the business world outside. From Glasgow, it was, and still is, easy to access the wonderful countryside so near to the city. Mountain climbing, luckily with expert friends, usually my good friend Christopher Brown and his brothers, Peter and Tony, was a great experience although often terrifying. However, I never excelled in any one sport – I tried them all! My chief claim to fame resulted from having very long legs. I could not run as fast as those with shorter legs, but when it came to jumping – Wow! I won the Glasgow University High Jump first time out and for the next four years. Oh no! I missed out on my Third Year there because I went to Loughborough College that summer for an Athletics Course. In trying the 'Western Roll' instead of my customary 'Scissors', I spiked my knee and was out of action for the University sports in that year.

In my final year, I failed to turn up regularly for training sessions at Westerlands, our sports ground. This infuriated the Athletics Section Captain and he dropped me from the team at the Inter University Sports at Aberdeen. However, I entrained with the boys at Buchanan Street Railway Station (of happy memory) and after being requested by my substitute to take his place, I jumped in the High Jump and won it outright! The Team Captain's decision not to give me a 'Blue' was overruled by the President, Mr. Roy Young, a wonderful old Surgeon in the Western Infirmary.

Of course, golf, tennis and partying persisted as before. I continued my annual Western Isles cruising right through University days with the Macleods of Taynuilt. The time eventually came for the Final Examination. I had worked as hard as I possibly could and felt confident up to a point, although realising that one also had to be lucky (unless one of the really clever ones). I <u>was</u> lucky, because I cannot ever recall just staring at an exam paper without having the remotest idea of the answer. What I did not know I made up, based on my long revision of first principles, especially in anatomy and physiology.

One evening the phone rang in Campbellfield, I answered it. "This is Professor Harrington speaking, could I speak to Doctor Walker?" I replied that there was no one of that name here. He went on, "It's a Dr. Percy Walker I want to speak to." I was thus spared the agony of fighting to see, or not to see, my name on the board in the Main Quadrangle the next day.

Commuting ~ Irvine to Glasgow

*T*ravelling daily by train from Irvine to Glasgow was worth recalling. I would be awakened around 6.00am by Mr. Martin, the Irvine Post Master, whose daughter, May Martin, was our (optimistic) piano teacher. "Peercie, it's time you were up!" In those days, you 'cawed a handle' to make the bell ring.

Margaret Gillespie, Jean McGinn's successor, would have sizzling plates of porridge and bacon and eggs on the *Esse* Cooker, which I would gobble before dashing the mile or so to the Station. There, my good friend the Booking Clerk (I wish I could remember his name!) would grab my bike, whilst I charged up the stairs to the 7.20 being held for me. As often as not, I would pitch head long into a smoke filled compartment, 8-a-side, with their mackintoshes spread over their knees, playing Solo Whist. Hopefully, I would land in a compartment, sometimes, near my good friend, Andrew Kay, later a famous Gastroenterologist Professor, who would look at my homework and make a few helpful suggestions without making it look too obvious.

Another memory of commuting from Irvine to Glasgow was on my violin lessons day when I was 'taught' by Miss Bessie Spence of the Scottish National Orchestra in the Athenaeum Hall. Practising on my violin was a certain way of getting a compartment to myself! Another time, I was left on my own after Paisley, on the way home, as I had spilt some beta hydroxybutiric acid on my new plus four suit, which had to be destroyed, sadly.

The violin referred to above, had the letters A.P.W. carved on it by my Uncle Percy, after whom I was called. Uncle Percy was a legend, killed just before World War One on one of Ayrshire's first motorbikes. The violin is now being cherished and played by Jessica, our Amanda's daughter.

In my latter years at University, instead of travelling daily from Irvine to Glasgow on the train, I lived in wonderful digs in 19 Bute Gardens, near the University. We were fed like fighting cocks by Mrs. McKie who charged us thirty shillings a week excluding weekends, when I either went home, or on climbing expeditions or sailing. A dark cloud, however, hung over us all during the late Thirties. Europe was being turned upside down by a man called Adolf Hitler.

I had been on a visit to Germany, by myself, in the summer of 1937. Even then, the German people were being mesmerised by this extraordinary man. They had suffered the humiliation of defeat and loss of territory after World War One. They were therefore easily roused to patriotism, which became a passionate desire to become 'Deutschland Uber Alles' again.

The First World War was, it seemed, to a large extent, the result of violent jealousy between the Royal Families of Europe, most noticeably between Kaiser Bill and his grandmother, our Queen Victoria, who herself ruled half the world. Hitler was the legacy of the awful events of 1914-18 and especially its aftermath.

I well recall a climbing weekend in Arran when we climbed every peak in two days. On that very weekend, we heard Neville Chamberlain telling us that as a result of his visit to Herr Hitler in Godesburg in Germany there "would be Peace in our Time." That was the summer of 1938. Neville Chamberlain, unwittingly, gave Britain time to get ready for the inevitability of war with Germany the following year. Hitler's Foreign Minister, Ribbentrop, however, after many visits to Britain, was convinced that Britain would never fight Germany. This encouraged Hitler to walk into Austria, then Poland, then Czechoslovakia, the Low Countries and eventually, Norway.

Climbing in Arran ~ 1938 ~ The A'chir Ridge
"There will be peace in our time" (Neville Chamberlain)

Qualifying

I qualified at Glasgow University on the very day that the Second World War broke out, September 3rd 1939. Chamberlain: "I gave an ultimatum to Herr Hitler that if he continued with his invasion plans in Europe, we would take whatever action would be necessary. No such assurance was received and consequently Great Britain is in a state of war with Germany."

Half a dozen of us, newly qualified doctors decided to go on a climbing trip in the Cuillins in Skye. Our main object was to attempt to climb every peak on the Cuillins, non-stop. This was quite an ambitious project. We stayed in a lovely little house in Glenbrittle, in the south of Skye owned by Mr. and Mrs. Chisholm who ran the Post Office from their house. I always remember Mr. Chisholm saying, "I hear the Chermans are at it again. I hope it's not as bad as the last time because I lost three brothers." We nearly succeeded in climbing 'the ridge in a day'. Sheer exhaustion brought us down from the mountaintops before we managed to climb the final peak, Sgur nan Gillean.

To revert to our qualifying: Over 200 or so newly qualified doctors, about 30 of them girls, assembled in the majestic Hunter Hall for the Graduation Ceremony. One memory of this occasion was a famous Army Lieutenant General, RAMC, optimistically telling us that he hoped that this 'show' would not be as bad as the previous one! I decided there and then not to join the army if I could help it. Nearly all my friends were in the Territorial Army, the Royal Air Force Volunteer Reserve or the Royal Naval Volunteer Reserve.

Climbing in the Cuillins, Skye ~ September 1939
"The Chermans are at it again."

I had been very disappointed when, in 1938, my application to join the RNVR as a final year medical student was turned down, there being no vacancies.

We were all ordered to Edinburgh Castle to register for National Service. Some of our very academic colleagues were earmarked for the Emergency Medical Service, 'EMS', staffing emergency hospitals, either purpose built or by modifying existing buildings, such as the super luxurious Turnberry Hotel (of many happy memories in my youth).

I had been earmarked for a career as a Dermatologist by the father of two good friends, Dr. A.D. Maclachlan, so I found myself house-man in the Skin Wards of the Western Infirmary. One patient who came to the Skin Ward before it closed was an Ordinary Seaman from *HMS Royal Oak*. He was in the ward with acute Pemphigus having come down from Thurso to Glasgow by train when he heard that the *Royal Oak* had been sunk with all hands lost in Scapa Flow, torpedoed by Oberleutnant Prien's U-Boat.

The 'powers that be' soon closed down the Skin Wards to make way for expected war casualties, so, although I worked in the out patient skin clinics, my chief job was in the Casualty Department.

One of my first recollections on the first Saturday night of the war was a procession of severe head injuries. It was a lottery whether I admitted these chaps since some were just drunk and others drunk with the additional complication of a fractured skull. However, we usually got it right, thanks to benign, experienced and kindly nursing staff.

Most of these casualties were caused by a total blackout of all streetlights and car lights (not to mention shuttered windows in all houses). The situation was somewhat eased by compulsory shades on car lights with the beams pointing directly downwards.

One day whilst working in the Casualty Department, a very bonny nurse who worked in the X-Ray Department said, "Percy, let's go in here into the linen cupboard and see what develops!" After a wee cuddle (only) Matron caught us when she came in to get some linen. "Go to your room at once Nurse, and as for you Doctor, I shall think about reporting you to the Medical Superintendent." "On second thoughts" she said, "don't do it again, I was young myself once!"

I remember Mrs. McKie in 19 Bute Gardens ordering her young medical guests in to the cellar as she said, "The Bosh are overhead" – in fact the flashes were from the tram cars in Byres Road!

Joining Up

*T*he war immediately changed everyone's lifestyle and a huge cloud hung over everything. It was difficult to imagine how our country could stop Hitler in his quest for domination of Europe with his overwhelming superiority of men and machines. Our country "Dug for Victory", tightened its belts and huge numbers of young and not so young ladies enrolled in munitions factories, the Land Army and as drivers of ambulances and service vehicles, as well as becoming WAAFs, ATS and WRNS. I became more and more conscious of the fact that amongst my non-medical friends, I was the odd man out, being in a 'reserved occupation'.

Having been told at Edinburgh Castle to await my call-up, I told them there that if it had to be the Army please may it be in a Scottish Regiment. The reply was, "Sir, in the Army you do what you're told, Sir!" This made me even more determined to get into the Navy, so one night I took the Sleeper from Kilmarnock to London (St. Enoch to St. Pancras) and on arrival in London, I met my Uncle Jimmie, one of the very few Territorial Brigadier Generals of World War One. He had a season ticket between Kilmarnock and London. I had told him of my mission and he had already arranged for an interview with Sir Harry, later Lord McGowan, in ICI House, Millbank. Sir Harry, a great friend of both my father and my uncle, received me very cordially, rang up the Medical Director General of the Navy, put me in a taxi to Naval Medical H.Q. I returned to Kilmarnock the same night, thirty shillings return, now a Temporary Acting Surgeon Lieutenant RNVR!

I was called up for the Army about a year later whilst serving in a destroyer at sea. I escaped Court Martial, however! By this time, the British Expeditionary Force was being driven to the channel ports by overwhelming numbers of the Wehrmacht who also had almost total air superiority. I was drafted to the Royal Naval Barracks in Chatham during the final days of Dunkirk, arriving there on 3rd June 1940. I was just too late to make a channel crossing – mixed feelings! But we did meet returning ships in the Medway, appallingly battered with the remains of some poor soldiers all over the decks.

Percy in Naval uniform ~ June 1940
Temporary Acting Surgeon Lieutenant RNVR

One evening I was talking to a young Officer in Chatham Barracks, who had made many trips of mercy. He told me we would never beat these damn Germans, but then Winston Churchill came on the radio: "We will fight them on the beaches we will fight them with whatever weapons we can find, we will NEVER surrender." Suddenly, the atmosphere in the Wardroom was transformed. Tattered and battered Officers stood up and cheered him to the echo. It was a turning point in the War and a great privilege to have been there at such a time.

Soon, I joined a queue of Medical Officers to be appointed to various ships or shore establishments. I recall asking the chap next to me what his name was and he said, "Watt," so I said, "We better change places, as I am 'Walker'." I went to *HMS Garth* and he went to *HMS Curacao*. His ship was sliced in two by the *Queen Mary* doing an anti-submarine zig-zag later in the War. Luck of the draw, but poor Watt.

Everywhere we went we had to have our gas masks at the ready, slung over our shoulders in a canvas container. These masks might have been effective against Chlorine and Phosgene of World War One, but I do not think that they would have been much use against biological warfare – a horrible threat now.

HMS Garth

HMS Garth was a split new Hunt Class Destroyer, one of the first of many of her class, just completed at John Brown's Yard, Clydebank.

HMS GARTH

I was due to join on a Saturday, but returning to the Western Infirmary from Chatham in my Naval uniform; quite a party ensued, so that when I woke up it was Sunday! I proceeded to Gourock as ordered. A Petty Officer said, "What ship, sir?" I said *Garth*. He said, "You're in trouble, lad, *Garth* sailed an hour ago!" But being a kindly man, as most Petty Officers are, he produced a fast Naval pinnace. I joined *Garth* at high speed just off Largs. Climbing up a ladder, I expected a reprimand, but the wonderful Captain, Lieutenant Commander Eric Hart Dyke, met me saying, "Welcome aboard Doc, jolly good of you to join us." Typical Navy!

I joined *Garth* on 26 June 1940 and was aboard until 7 August 1941. We were doing sea trials on the measured mile when we received a signal to proceed 'with all dispatch' to a position off the north coast of Ireland. A terrible sight awaited us. A huge oil slick with innumerable bodies bobbing up and down as if to say "Good morning, good morning." All dead Italians with broken necks, as they had jumped with their life jackets on. They were rounded up from Italian cafés in Scotland – a black day, terrible for these lovable people who had become such good friends of Scotland. The Blue Star Liner *Arandora Star* had been torpedoed by a U-Boat, with Italian internees bound for Canada. We returned to our base chastened. I was seasick to the point of being almost unconscious during our dash to the scene of the sinking. I wondered how I would survive this much longer. It was my 24th Birthday I remember.

Soon, we went to Scapa Flow in the Orkneys to 'work up'. We visited lots of lovely places on the way to Scapa (and back) so I did not miss my Western Isles cruise in 1940.

Memories of Scapa

*M*y memories of Scapa Flow included the huge battleships, some survivors of the First World War, some later, like *Rodney, Nelson, Valiant, Hood, Renown, Repulse*, the *Royal Oak* – the *Royal Oak* was already at the bottom in Scapa Flow. The destroyers were at their base, Lyness on the Island of Hoy, an enormous base with a massive number of troops, some for defence, others training for overseas campaigns yet to come. I remember an ENSA concert in the huge hall in Lyness where Evelyn Laye captivated the troops. She was a great old trouper, a forerunner of Vera Lynn.

Our activities at Scapa were mainly working up exercises, getting the ship and the ship's company, shipshape. At sea, we would try out our Asdic anti-submarine echo-sounding device. I was employed as the Asdic Officer, which required me to work 'The Plot'. This device plotted the course, position and speed of our ship and most importantly, sent up echo signals to The Plot from the seabed or from submerged objects. We practised with our own submarines. One day we had a strong echo. There were no friendly submarines in the area. I was excited, naturally, and yelled up the voice pipe to the Bridge, "Object bearing so and so, depth so and so." We raced to the spot but the echo got weaker and weaker. "You stupid boy," the Captain said. I had inadvertently given him a directly reciprocal bearing! Lucky U-boat! However, I was equally lucky in another destroyer, a couple of years later when a torpedo's wake approached us, but passed right under us.

Another duty as a M.O. was, most importantly, Officer in Charge of Wines and Spirits. We were supplied with only the best from Saccone and Speed at duty free prices, so at today's price, a bottle of whisky would just be about a pound sterling. I was also in charge of the Confidential Books, which were updated on a daily basis by Cipher signals. Our Petty Officer Telegraphist handled all signals that were not either Secret or Top Secret. I had to decipher the latter because of my 'officer' status – strange! I recall one Most Top Secret cipher – "It is anticipated that Great Britain will soon be at war with France." France had fallen and Britain simply had to prevent Hitler taking over their assets for use against us. The great Charles de Gaulle must have been horrified at the attitude of some of his fellow Frenchmen. He had a large following of Free French in Britain. They and the French Underground Resistance represented the true spirit of France.

Most signals came by radio, but ship to shore was by Aldis Lamp, i.e. Morse signalling during periods of wireless silence.

I had another job, censoring the lower deck letters. This was a detestable job. Letters from the sailors to their loved ones were very intimate and often very poignant, such as when Devonport was being blitzed – and we were a Devonport ship. My examination of the letters was just a rapid check to see that no one had mentioned where we were, or where we were going to and such like.

The doctor was an important link between the Wardroom, the Petty Officers and the Seamen, so it was essential to demonstrate complete confidentiality of censorship.

After about a month in Scapa, we proceeded in early August 1940, down the West Coast of Britain, the intention being that our ship should become a convoy escort in the Atlantic. It was very soon discovered that Hunt Class Destroyers, certainly the early ones, were not good sea boats in the Atlantic swell. So we were dispatched with all speed to join the 21st Destroyer Flotilla based at Sheerness in the Medway.

At the time of Dunkirk and its immediate aftermath, the destroyer flotillas based at ports such as Harwich, Sheerness and Dover took a terrible pasting, with heavy losses. The new Hunts were a very welcome addition to these depleted flotillas whose survivors were mainly the old V and W Class, some of them veterans of the First World War. The Hunts had an enormous advantage in that their main armament, 4" guns, were high angle guns, whereas the V and Ws were designed to combat surface vessels, before dive-bombers were invented.

After Dunkirk, with the enemy lining the entire coast of Europe from Norway to the Spanish border, it was deemed impossible for ships to bring supplies from USA and Canada to Britain, especially London, via the Western Approaches, i.e. from the Atlantic directly up the English Channel. So all supplies had to be routed round the north of Scotland and down the East Coast, assuming that they had been lucky enough to escape the U-boat menace in the Atlantic. This obviously required anti-submarine forces all along the northern and eastern seaboards of Britain. RAF Coastal Command played a vital anti-submarine role, as well as our naval forces.

The merchant ships of all ages, shapes and sizes, having survived the Atlantic, converged in the Firth of Forth off a town called Methil in Fife. From here, convoys were grouped and escorted by Rosyth/Humber destroyers where they were met by Harwich or Sheerness destroyers that took them into the Thames Estuary.

Off East Anglia, the North Sea is very shallow, some banks, such as Dogger Bank, can clear above water at exceptionally low tides. The navigable channels, both northbound and southbound, 'The Tramlines' as they were called, were marked by buoys. These channels were swept day and night by gallant minesweepers, mostly converted fishing vessels, usually skippered by RNVR officers. The shallow North Sea did not permit submarine, i.e. U-Boat, activity.

East Coast Convoy ~ 1940

The Germans, of course, became adept at laying mines, magnetic and later acoustic, along the paths of the convoys, and they could pick off the merchant ships by firing torpedoes from their Schnellbooten (E-Boats), so the East Coast destroyers had to guard their flock against E-Boats and dive-bombers as best they could. The awful Junkers 87 dive-bombers were very chary of taking to the air after our wonderful RAF Fighter Command, 'The Few', gained air superiority in the Battle of Britain, which was raging when *Garth* arrived at Sheerness.

I recall when we were given shore leave whilst our ship was having a breather in harbour one glorious Sunday afternoon and I took a bus to visit old friends, the Browns – Christopher's parents, in Kent.

Upon arrival at their lovely home, a tennis party was in full swing. The sky was dotted with Spitfires and Hurricanes versus Messerschmits – this was one of the RAF Fighter Command's greatest days. On return to Sheerness, I was made aware of a General Recall to all ships – an invasion scare?

Our flotilla was ordered to sea with all dispatch, and I luckily got aboard in time to unlock the safe containing all the Confidential Books, including cipher codes. I had the keys with me, as I was supposed to carry them with me at all times – but possibly not when on shore leave! All these books had to be chucked over the side in weighted steel boxes – goodbye to all my homework! For a reason that is still conjectural, Hitler did not attempt to send his invasion force (Operation Sea Lion) across the channel.

The heavy cruisers *Aurora* and *Galatea* had already left the Thames area and retreated to northern harbours for safety. So the 21st Destroyer Flotilla and 'Dad's Army' seemed to be all that could stop Hitler coming across the Channel to the south coast of England. I believe that Goering's Luftwaffe must have been demoralised by our fighter pilots, especially after they had had all their own way at Dunkirk. Thank God for the RAF!

I think on that Sunday in September 1940, our fighters brought down 183 enemy planes, with many losses of their own, of course.

Our job of escorting the convoys meant leaving harbour at any time of the day or night according to tides and the state of readiness of the convoys. Ships, up to 30 or so in a convoy, were themselves under the command of a retired Royal Navy Commodore, usually a senior officer who volunteered to do it all again!

The escorts took station, usually abreast or astern of the merchant ships, keeping a sharp lookout for E Boats and bombers.

One early morning, returning to Sheerness having seen our convoy safely up the Thames Estuary, I was having breakfast in the wardroom when an almighty bang seemed to make our ship jump out of the water. Our fellow ship in that convoy, an old V and W class, *HMS Venetia*, had been blown apart by an acoustic mine just astern of us. The device seemed to have been set to detonate after the ship ahead had passed over it. We were a ship ahead because our Captain was senior to *Venetia*'s!

I was ordered into the motorboat where I met a very distinguished RN veteran Captain Cordeaux. He and his small boats from ashore and our motor boat had picked up a few survivors, but most of the crew of *HMS* Venetia were trapped below in the bow and stern sections – with the middle of the ship being blown apart. It was terrible to see comrades trapped inside. The scuttles, or portholes, were too small to permit escape – this was rectified later, I believe. The explosion, so near us, did superficial damage, but did not prevent us going to sea.

On one convoy, we did sustain quite serious damage by running aground. I remember at my Action Station (we were always at Action Stations in these waters) I heard a crunching noise unlike anything I had heard before. On reaching the Bridge to see what was happening, I saw Yarmouth Pier within spitting distance. Our navigator, a charming young man, did not please their Lordships and left us soon afterwards. This incident gave *Garth* a spell ashore in a dry dock at Tilbury. This respite proved to be far less safe than being in the North Sea! One lovely afternoon, I remember seeing the sky black with huge numbers of Heinkel, Dorniers and Junkers – the first of the daylight raids on London. The West End got a terrible pasting that day. Some of us went up to town the next day and the wreckage was indescribable. When we returned from the West End to the East End, where our ship was, we discovered that the East End had the received same treatment – ghastly!

We saw a Luftwaffe bomber with both engines on fire just seconds before hitting the ground near us. The rear gunner, knowing that his number was up, decided to take somebody with him. He spattered our upper deck with bullets. I just looked on, glued to the spot. My two sailor companions ran for their lives; one was hit in the ankle and the other was killed – our first casualty so far. My motto, "When in doubt, do nothing" still holds good!

On returning from shore leave in the trot boat one evening, we were transferring some sailors from *Campbell* back onto their ship, and on passing the porthole of *Campbell*'s Captain, Captain Mark Pizey, RN, one of our lot said, "Get some sea time in, Pizey." Captain Pizey was later knighted when he, in *Campbell*, played a gallant part versus *Scharnhorst*, *Gneisenau* and *Prinz Eugen* in their dash up the Channel. *HMS Campbell*, Flotilla Leader of the 21st Destroyer Flotilla, did not often go to sea on routine convoys, hence the more regular seagoing sailor's jibes!

Some convoys were more peaceful than others. At one time, apart from our flotilla leader *HMS Campbell*, we were the only destroyer, for a few days, able to go to sea.

HMS Garth, with, I think, three sister Hunts were involved in an operation, 'Operation Lucid'. The idea was to tow the old 'flat iron', *HMS Erebus*, a Monitor, which was an old cruiser, stripped of upper works, but with 15" guns mounted on her deck. She was being towed across the channel with the object of bombarding and softening up Boulogne Harbour, after which two ancient merchantmen were to sail into the harbour – *War Nizam* and another ship whose name I forget. These two ships, full of high explosives, were to be abandoned by the skeleton crew and blown up in the harbour by remote control. As far as I remember, *Erebus'* tugs could not get her into position, so the whole operation was called off. *Garth* actually ran aground off the cliffs of France, but the German searchlights were looking further out to sea and we escaped unscathed!

We had a change of routine once or twice. Instead of escorting East Coast convoys, we took a small number of merchantmen through the Straits of Dover to Portsmouth and back. I think that this was purely for propaganda purposes. We learnt afterwards that Winston Churchill was watching us from the White Cliffs of Dover together with Pathé Gazette cameras. The Straits are only about 20 miles across, so we were easily in the range of the massive German guns on Cap Gris Nez.

One time, a salvo from Cap Gris Nez fell just short of our port side and the next, seconds later, just beyond our starboard side. Our skipper decided not to alter course. If we <u>had</u> done, we would have had a direct hit from salvo No. 3, I suspect. Our Captain on the way home, cleared lower deck and held a prayer of thanksgiving for our survival. Some of our ship's company called him a 'Bible Thumper', but most were glad to join in the prayers! (I certainly was!)

Three days at sea and one in the harbour was our usual routine; we tied up alongside several other destroyers for our day in harbour. We were never very temperate on those occasions! If time permitted, we joined up with Wrens for a run ashore – great fun, lovely girls! Sheerness, in those days was not a holiday resort, but a rather dingy Officers Club was a haven of rest!

I remember saying to myself that the citizens of our country could be divided into those who could reasonably anticipate survival and those who think that a week is a long time.

During my time in *Garth*, I was conscious of the fact that my medical knowledge was mainly theoretical, having not done my postgraduate training after qualifying. Luckily, British seamen are a wonderfully healthy lot, so I never had to make a very learned diagnosis. What I did learn was to appreciate the effects of stress and boredom and separation on people – a great lesson in appreciating psychosomatic disorders later when in General Practice.

Our Chief Engineer Officer, Alec Hobden, a veteran of World War One when he joined the Navy as a Stoker, joined *Garth* on his first commission as a two stripe Lieutenant (E) (for Engineer), RN. His yarns in the darkened Wardroom, red lights only for instant night vision, were wonderful, if repetitive. I kept him going by slightly cooking the wine books to give him his necessary tots of Coates Plymouth gin without which he would have gone mad sooner, poor chap. He had to be invalided out, completely shattered, a while later.

One night, on the 20 November 1940, off the East Coast, we encountered an E-boat in our searchlights. We were one of the very first of HM ships ever to be fitted with RADAR. We had an RNVR boffin on board, a very untypical sailor, but nevertheless, a good shipmate. He spent his days and nights in a sealed compartment with his Top Secret paraphernalia. Maybe it was this Lieutenant Coates who honed us on to the E-boat? At any rate, we got him, or her, in our sights before she got us. We fired all we had at her. As we drew close, we could see dead and dying all over the shattered craft. We launched our whaler and picked up survivors, some terribly wounded. It seemed odd, killing people one minute and seconds later, risking our own lives in a stationary ship – a sitting duck for another E-boat! The Wardroom was suddenly a hospital, full of wounded Germans.

By an extraordinary coincidence, our E-boat was encountered on the very day that *Bismarck* was sunk in far northern waters. The E-boat Captain, mortally wounded, was still alert enough to hear on the radio "The *Bismarck* has been sunk." "Propaganda!" he said, "The *Bismarck* is unsinkable"! As he died, he said to me "Hold my hand, I am dying, I love England." He earlier had said how much he had enjoyed his holidays in England pre-war.

My wartime papers revealed that this E-boat Captain's name was Ober Leutnant Hans Detlefsin. We picked up five badly wounded survivors and seven in reasonably good shape. Our chaps in the lower deck were very kind and hospitable to those who a few minutes earlier tried to kill us, and us them. One officer in the E-boat was a different kettle of fish. He said he was the ship's doctor. In fact, he was a 'died in the wool' SS Nazi of the most unpleasant type possible. I offered him a glass of water. He spat it out and said, "Give me Cognac." I did not! We rammed and sunk the E-boat once all the survivors were off. Lt. Cdr. Hart Dyke possibly hoped for a DSC after the action. In fact, the poor chap was reprimanded as Their Lordships wanted to inspect an E-boat alive and all that was therein.

BISMARK survivors
~ 20 Nov 1940
(newspaper cutting)

Survivors from the *Bismarck.*

I re-read an amazingly researched book, 'The Battle of the East Coast 1939-1945' by J.P. Foynes. On page 94, the author stated that *HMS Campbell* was the E-boat's killer. When I wrote to him saying that it was *HMS Garth*, belonging to the flotilla of which *Campbell* was the Leader, he graciously apologised for his error.

Another change from interminable convoy duties – whilst on escort duties, *Garth* and *Eglinton* were ordered to proceed to the Texel, off the coast of Holland. A report had been received that a fleet of German vessels had left the Zuider Zee.

The 20th Destroyer Flotilla ships *HMS Esk*, *HMS Express* and *HMS Ivanhoe*, based at Immingham, were dispatched to the area. *Esk* blew up on a mine and sank immediately. *HMS Express*, severely damaged, was later towed back home to base by *HMS Jupiter*, the Fifth Flotilla Leader, under the command of Lord Louis Mountbatten. *Ivanhoe* was seriously damaged. When *Garth* arrived on the scene, *Esk* had sunk, *Ivanhoe* was sinking, having been torpedoed by one of our own M.T.B.s, which had picked up her Captain and other survivors. *Ivanhoe's* Captain, I'm sure, was the same officer to whom I was talking in Chatham Barracks when Winston Churchill made his rousing speech – I remember him telling me the name of his ship. The report of the German ships sailing from Holland turned out to be false. One of our air patrols had actually spotted a coastal convoy of fairly harmless merchant ships and mistook them for men o' war. So *Garth* and *Eglinton* sailed for home as quickly as we could. I think *Eglinton* beat us home, but on the way a Blohm and Voss seaplane circled round *Garth*. We expected to be surrounded by bombers intent on finishing us off, but they never came. Mountbatten was reported as saying later that the Blohm and Voss aircrew were maybe not Nazis!

RM Group MNBDO(2)

I eventually received papers telling me that my time in *Garth* was up and that my 'relief' would soon be arriving to take my place. I was drafted to Portsmouth Barracks, *HMS Victory*, to await my next appointment. This was August 1941, during which time I was allowed shore leave at home. *Garth's* Captain, Lt.Cdr. Eric Hart Dyke, was relieved just before me, so I had a few weeks serving with her new Captain, Lt. Cdr. J.P. Scratchard, RN. It was customary for Their Lordships not to keep their doctors too long in the one place, so I left the ship that had been my home for 1¼ years with very mixed feelings. I was glad to leave behind the North Sea but NOT such wonderful shipmates.

During my time in *Garth*, I managed a few periods of leave, when I went home. I met many friends in the Territorial Army who had been in the Services long before I had, but who had yet to taste enemy action. Their time came though!

Many of my friends, in addition to the 'Family gunners', were in the Glasgow Highlanders Battalion of the Highland Light Infantry, as well as the 602 City of Glasgow Squadron, Royal Air Force Volunteer Reserve.

I was subsequently drafted to a Royal Marine Unit, called RM Group MNBDO(2), i.e. Marine Naval Base Defence Organisation (2). There was already a (1) overseas in the Mediterranean. I joined this outfit on 12 December 1941. I could have done with a spell in a Naval Hospital to learn a bit about my trade a bit better, but that is not the way of Their Lordships.

I arrived at MNBDO(2) Headquarters in a lovely country house, Bentworth, near Alton, Hampshire. We were accommodated in tents in the grounds of this stately home and had a life of luxury for a week or so. Eventually, we – i.e. a squad of RNVR Medical Officers – were dispersed to various parts of the country. I went first to Eypemouth, near Bridport, Dorset, and then to Devon and Cornwall. The Scilly Isles were also in my parish.

I was Medical Officer in charge of anti-aircraft batteries manned by Royal Marines. These gun sites were situated on the most remote headlands on the west coast peninsula. As I could not be in more than one place at once, I evolved a plan for the isolated Marines to report to the nearest Army or RAF station for medical advice whenever required. This worked admirably and I spent carefree days zooming around the beautiful West Country on my Norton 500cc Motorbike collecting and collating information about the sick or wounded for whom I was responsible. This was necessary because Their Lordships stuck rigidly to the necessity of 'The Medical Officer's Journal'. This had to be kept meticulously. I think promotion depended on it. I was never promoted!

Our medical equipment was equally quaint. We were supplied with medical chests, complete with various gallipots of ingredients for making up mixtures and powders, with neat little scales and the necessary measuring glasses. Ideal for peacetime perhaps a century earlier!

One Sunday afternoon, I was having a pint or two in the Royal Hotel in Truro when a gaggle of staff cars arrived at the pub, and in trooped the 'top brass' of the Royal Marines who were due to take lunch there. A charming, very senior Marine Officer, festooned with red and gold, said, "Hello, Doc, how's it going?" I explained what I was doing. "Jolly good," he said, "I hope you are enjoying it." Having had a pint, or three, by this time, I said that I found the life a bit monotonous. "Good," he said, "I shall send a car for you at six o'clock this evening when I shall arrange something more exciting for you!"

That night I joined Lt.Cdr. Peter Scott's Steam Gunboat, *HMS Wild Goose*. Peter Scott of *Wild Fowl* fame was also determined to be as famous as his father, Scott of the Antarctic! I had no such ambitions! We left our moorings in, if I remember rightly, Poole Harbour. Peter Scott told us that we were having a jaunt across the Channel to Guernsey, there to pick up a few Germans and bring them back with us! What a pity a steam pipe fractured on the way across and we had to be towed back to harbour!

HMS Menace

*A*fter this episode, about twenty or so Medical Officers, all RNVR, were sent to Portsmouth Barracks as a 'pool' for Combined Operations trips. We were certainly not handpicked or specially trained Commandos although someone suggested that we might be put through some 'toughening up' training. I seem to remember walking and running miles and then walking out to sea to clamber on board landing craft that then emptied us back into the sea.

Some of my colleagues were sent to the Western Isles and Lochs of Scotland. Lucky chaps! Troon Golf Club was Combined Operations Headquarters! I was very envious of them, but had to content myself in Barracks wondering what was coming next; total boredom followed by frantic excitement. About this time I was drafted to something called *HMS Menace*.

A raid on the Lofoten Islands, high up in the Arctic off the Norwegian Coast, had already taken place. With incredible gallantry, but only limited success, it was, it seems, decided to do it again. We were given Arctic gear, white survival suits, and I saw my first string vest. Of all places to find myself in was, in top secret circumstances, to be in the King's Arms Hotel in Irvine, my native town! I was sitting round a table in a well-guarded upper room and Lord Lovat of 4th Commando fame was briefing his troops when a roar of anger went up – the whole show was cancelled. Somebody had talked!

One result of being in *HMS Menace* was that we were ordered to put our pay, or most of it, into our Bank, i.e. making an 'allotment', there being little facilities for spending money in the

Lofotens. I forgot to cancel my allotment, so, for the next three or four years, I was drawing full pay plus the allotment money in the Clydesdale Bank, Irvine. I never noticed or enquired why I was so rich until the Admiralty Paymasters found out. It was later, whilst in the Far East, I became as poor as I had been rich, due to monthly deductions from my pay. I was eventually let off the remaining debt, about £300, upon demobilisation.

I returned to Portsmouth Barracks after my holiday at home, or at least, in my native town. I had been under strict orders not to walk the mile or so to my family home whilst in H.Q. King's Arms, Irvine, for about one day!

Combined Ops.

Our next excitement was participating in the notorious Dieppe Raid, in summer 1942.

The Allied War leaders had decided to try out a frontal assault on an enemy held coast by landing huge numbers of troops, tanks etc. by either amphibious craft or landing craft. The latter would run up a beach and lower the forward ramp doors to allow troops and vehicles ashore. Too bad if the craft could not get near enough to the beach!

One day our gang was sent to the Admiralty in London for a briefing for this operation. The original idea was to send a gun-boat, *HMS Locust*, into Dieppe Harbour where a demolition party would blow up installations, get back on board – and, then what? I think MLs (Motor Launches) were to be around if *Locust* could not move out. As usual, their Lordships thought that having an officer with a red stripe between his gold braid would be a good idea. I do not recall having any training for this 'derring do' or being issued with anything like the adequate medical equipment. I drew the Joker in the pack and was appointed to sail across in *Locust*. Later, it was decided to put me in an ML accompanying *Locust*. However, again somebody talked! I was in a crowded bar in the Queen's Hotel in Southsea near Portsmouth one night, when some poor officer mouthed the word 'Dieppe'. He was quickly escorted away. I never did hear what his fate was, and the operation was postponed for a few weeks.

I was one of many in a huge dockside hall on Newhaven Pier (from which port one sails to Dieppe in peacetime). The place was full of Canadians who had been cooped up in Southern England and were raring to go. A film was shown that night: 'The Warsaw Concerto'. The evocative music still gives an all too vivid impression of the Germans invading Poland. A day or two later, the killed, wounded and captured outnumbered the survivors.

The second time round, the real thing, was on 19 August 1942. This time, I was allocated a Tank Landing Craft. There were no tanks on board, only two doctors and several sick bay attendants with, this time, transfusion sets (plasma). Of course, we had our standard medical chests – 'Ships for the use of' – as well. We had a grandstand view of the awful battles ashore. Troops were mown down as they jumped ashore; vehicles were bogged down and blown up. The 3rd and 4th Commandos were successful in scaling the cliffs on either side of the harbour and with the utmost bravery silenced many German guns.

Somebody reckoned that to send the ambulance tank landing craft ashore would be futile in the midst of such chaos, so we were told to go home.

The RAF, as usual, had done wonderful work in the air, keeping enemy bombers at bay, more or less, but many of our ships, including *HMS Berkeley*, *Garth*'s sister ship, were hit and sunk by shore batteries or aircraft. I still do not know why our support landing craft did not make an attempt to get inshore to try to save men on the beach or in the water, but sadly, I don't think it would have been a worthwhile operation.

On the way home, I was sunning myself on the tarpaulin covering the landing craft hangar when two aircraft flew over. As we were almost within swimming distance of our white cliffs, I thought that they must be ours. They were Messerschmits 110s! One dropped a bomb, which hit the landing craft beside us. The bomb did not explode, but went right through the bottom of the hull.

The vessel started to sink, so we lashed ourselves to it and successfully beached both craft. I was able to purloin the contents of my medical chest with an easy conscience. I still have the sphygmomanometer and the auroscope.

Amazingly, not one of our gang of MOs had been damaged. One, Myles Patrick Martin, who came from Ballinteer near Aileen's hometown, Dundrum in Dublin, was awarded an immediate DSO, rescuing and treating people from the sea whilst his destroyer was under intense fire.

My next and final participation in the Combined Ops. was to take part in 'Operation Torch'. This was a massive undertaking. Liners from all over world, i.e. the world that was on our side, foregathered in the Clyde, off Greenock. We sailed, I think, on 1st November 1942. Pearl Harbour had already taken place on 7th November 1941. The United States of America, taken completely by surprise, lost huge numbers of lives and ships, and, without further ado, pledged themselves to free the world of Nazi and Japanese aggression.

The Allied forces in South East Asia were outnumbered and outgunned, both on land and sea. At this time we lost *HMS Repulse* and *HMS Prince of Wales* off the East Coast of Malaya.

Thousands of British and Commonwealth troops, having survived these battles, suffered terrible privations and cruelty in the Japanese Prisoner of War Camps. Hong Kong was also overrun by the Japs and the suffering there was unbelievable.

Operation
Torch

M.V. Sobieski and Operation Torch

*T*o get back to Operation Torch – our great liners were jam-packed with American troops. We slipped from our moorings one November evening in 1942, and the following morning, I looked out of the porthole in my cabin and recognised Inveraray. The idea apparently was to confuse Hitler as to our intentions. I was aboard the Flagship of the Polish Mercantile Marine, *MV Sobieski*, named after a great Polish patriot.

Eventually, we were underway, bound for North Africa. The idea was to fight Rommel in the West, as well as in the East of North Africa.

We reluctantly, and very sadly, had to take care of the French Fleet in case Hitler got hold of it after the fall of France. General Charles de Gaulle had made it to England with his Free French troops, but the Vichy French, led by Admiral Darlan and Marshall Petain, paradoxically the Victor of Verdun in the 1914-1918 War, were in favour of giving in to Hitler in order to avoid further destruction of their beloved France.

The enormous convoy sailed unscathed through the Bay of Biscay and into the Mediterranean. On passage, I was conscious of the fact that alcohol was taboo when American troops were on board. However, my friend the Polish Purser in *Sobieski* indicated that the British Board of Trade Regulations (we were under their aegis) permitted one bottle of spirits per day per person in the Sick Bay. I pointed this out to a very nice American 4-Star General, our senior officer of American Troops. "Fill that Sick Bay, Doc!" he said – I did! With the finest possible cognac and wine aboard, it was much less traumatic landing in Algiers for these chaps.

At first, the French fired on our troops, but after all or nearly all had landed, they called it a day and were almost welcoming.

I had to remain on board as Senior Medical Officer, but I became a bit restless and decided to have my first look at Algiers. My colleague on board, Surgeon Lt. Ron Tipple, and some of our Sick Berth Attendants, lowered a ship's lifeboat and we propelled ourselves by hand power into Algiers Harbour. We had a quick look round this ancient place and were testing the local brew copiously, when suddenly, everyone was ordered back to their ships. We leapt onto a 'Trot Boat' and returned to the *Sobieski*. For years, the Captain must have wondered what had become of one of his lifeboats!

The Germans suddenly appeared overhead and did a horrible amount of damage to our ships and escorts. The main body consisting of the liners was ordered back to UK as quickly as possible and were, in consequence, completely unescorted. A lot of beautiful luxury liners on their way home were sent to the bottom by U-Boats. We escaped, rumour having it that our Polish Captain knew a thing or two about U-boats!

HMS Southdown

Soon after my return to the UK, whilst I was hanging around in Barracks again, Their Lordships sent me back to where I had started. I think it was because I said I wanted to see the world in far off places. So, I found myself back in East Coast Convoys in *HMS Southdown*, another Hunt Class Destroyer, but this time with the 16th Destroyer Flotilla in Harwich. Life, going up and down the 'Tramlines', was very similar to life in *Garth*. In both cases, we had very 'happy ships' in *Garth* and *Southdown*. In the Royal Navy, a happy ship is an efficient ship, brought about by mutual trust and everyone knowing one's job – a good blueprint for our Country. I shared this sentiment with my very good friend, the late John Mott, Captain, R.N.

We had the same excitement and routines as in my *Garth* experiences, possibly not quite so frequently or intensively, as the threat of invasion had receded and we now had air superiority.

One vivid memory is of the Bomber Command Lancasters and Halifaxes winging their way to targets in Germany on a nightly basis, and sometimes, enormous flights of US Air force Bombers doing the same thing by day.

I referred earlier to a torpedo being seen to have passed under *Southdown* – fortunately, a miscalculation of our draught by an E-boat.

By now, the Italian Campaign had started and the job in hand was to kick the Germans out of Italy, having got the better of them in such places as Alamein, Tobruk and Tunisia.

Southdown was earmarked for the Mediterranean and we were all told to have our 'Whites' ready. For some reason, still unknown to me, we were left behind to continue to plod up and down the North Sea, whilst, I think, 3 *Hunts* from our flotilla took part in the Salerno and Anzio landings.

I remember proceeding to sea one day from Harwich, and I woke up in what I thought were not too familiar surroundings. We had been tied up at Parkstone Quay, alongside another Hunt, *HMS Eglinton*. It seems that I had turned in, in the Eglinton Sick Bay cot whilst the Eglinton doctor did likewise in my bed. A signal from *Eglinton* to *Southdown* leaving harbour: "We have your doctor, do you have ours"? I think, "Don't make it a habit, doctor," was as far as my reprimand got!

HMS SOUTHDOWN

It was sometimes possible to make the journey all the way up to Rosyth and once we were due to arrive at Rosyth on New Year's Eve. The Scottish sailors found the temptation too much and leapt off the ship, making for Dunfermline Station. A very serious situation. Commander in Chief, Rosyth, told the law-abiding ship's company to take whatever action they thought fit against the miscreants, who had been rounded up and sent back to their ship. We spent the first few days of the year swinging round a buoy in the Firth of Forth with all shore leave cancelled!

One bonus was to sail from Rosyth to the Shetland Isles by ourselves, just for a holiday. It was a lovely break from the monotonous tramlines.

I left *Southdown* just before the *Scharnhorst, Gneisenau* and *Prinz Eugen* made a break for freedom. These three great ships of the German High Seas Fleet had been in the Atlantic since 1941, doing enormous damage to Allied shipping. Hitler wanted them safely back in German ports, so a gamble was taken to run them through the Channel and the Straits of Dover. Our destroyers and our Fleet Air Arm Swordfish were, due to bad luck, bad weather and some sad mistakes on the part of interpretation of Radar and RAF intelligence, unable to stop these ships reaching their destination, although the 21st and 16th Destroyer flotillas did themselves proud, as did the Fleet Air Arm. The enemy ships were sufficiently damaged to have them undergo lengthy repairs.

Sometime previously, the *Tirpitz* was severely disabled in a Norwegian Fjord by our incredibly gallant midget submariners, one of whom was Cdr. John Lorimer, DSO, now residing in Ayrshire and a good friend.

Disabling these ships of the German Navy was, with 'the Battle of Britain', decisive in winning the battle of the Atlantic and subsequent victory.

My year or so in *Southdown* was a mixture of fun, fear and friendships.

Parkstone Quay was a very social place in spite of the daily comings and goings of war. The Harwich Wrens were a particularly splendid lot, especially the ratings who tended to be more high born and affectionate than the Wren Officers. I suppose the officers bore more responsibility, which was, understandably, an inhibiting factor. The Senior Officers ashore, men of very high

70

rank, had a very commendable camaraderie with the Wren ratings that, of course, would have been outrageous in either the Army or Air Force.

We had a lovely Officers Club at a nearby country house – Michaelstowe. It was a great safety valve to repair there for a good meal, good drinks and to fraternise with other ship's companies and, of course, Wrens!

Amongst our ship's great friends was Lieutenant Nicholas Monserrat of (later) *Cruel Sea* fame, who commanded a Harwich corvette. Our Captain, James Marjoribanks, later married one the Harwich Wrens, Jean Lyle. These girls were a memorable lot and really good friends. I never managed to contact any of them post war except for Jean. Later, she married General Jack Frost, of Arnhem Red Beret fame, both of whom I met years later at Lucy Knox's Wedding.

Southdown wardroom was a very happy place. I used to tease Lt. Fanshawe, later Lt.Cdr. Fanshawe, our next Captain after Marjoribanks, by saying that I was a Lieutenant before he was. *Southdown's* First Lieutenant was Lt. Anson, RN. Eddie was exceedingly popular on board with the sailors and his fellow officers. Eton Public School entry into the Navy, the son of the Earl of Lichfield, he moved with what now might be called 'Sloane Rangers' in his social life and, in today's parlance, would no doubt be called 'laid back'. One day, returning to our ship after a run ashore, Eddie fell off the gangplank. He died immediately from a fractured skull. We all went to his funeral at the family seat, Shugborough Hall near Lichfield, where Eddie's grave is in the ancestral graveyard.

I cannot recall much more about life in *Southdown* apart from well-known routine convoys and the inevitable sinkings of merchant ships. The E Boats were much more inclined to attack the merchantmen than their escorts.

Michaelstowe Officers' Club ~ Harwich 1943
Lt Eddie Anson RN, Wren Patricia Rambaut, Lt Cdr Nicholas
Monserrat RNVR, Wren Liz Macdonnell

After a total of nearly three years during the Battle of the East Coast, I was infinitely luckier than most to get through it all without any personal damage, and to avoid horrendous events in both ships – in the case of the *Garth*, after I left, and in the case of *Southdown*, before I joined.

Before leaving my tales of the North Sea and the convoys in the Atlantic, I must mention the Liberty Ships designed and built by man called 'Kaiser' in American shipyards. Without this 'bridge over the Atlantic', these merchantmen, full of the machinery of war, not to mention thousands of American troops who augmented our attenuated forces, I cannot see how the War could ever have ended in our favour. There was no way that the Allies could have succeeded in removing the Nazi curse from the world without the help of the Americans, both on land and sea and in the air. I also think that subsequent generations should always be reminded of the Battle of the East Coast and, just as important, the terrible damage inflicted on coastal towns on the East Coast of England while these battles were raging.

HMS Daedalus and SS Stratheden

*M*y next appointment was to *HMS Daedalus*, Lee on Solent, across the harbour from Portsmouth in November 1943. Again, I was in a pool of Medical Officers – this time destined for the Far East. I did a course in *Daedalus* in Aeronautical Medicine, which was concerned with such matters as the effect of oxygen depletion on pilot's skills and judgments. In an oxygen-depleted chamber, it was amazing to look at one's handwriting and verbal nonsense that was recorded for us to see and hear later.

I was sent to both the London School of Tropical Medicine and the Liverpool School of Tropical Medicine. The duplication was somebody's mistake, but I did not complain. Both courses were most interesting and helpful later. I could tell the difference (and still can) between various species of mosquito and their life cycles in relation to Malaria and Yellow Fever and other diseases.

Soon, in November 1943, I received a 'Draft Chit' to proceed overseas. Together, with a dozen or so RNVR Medical Officers, I embarked on the P&O Liner *Stratheden* at Gourock. I said good-bye to my father on Irvine platform. Little did I think that this really was goodbye. He died about a year later of cancer of the oesophagus – a particularly unpleasant terminal disease.

The trip from Gourock to Alexandria, through the Bay of Biscay and the Mediterranean, was uneventful as far as enemy encounters were concerned, the battles having moved from North Africa to Italy. We had a brief refuelling stop at Gibraltar where I did a quick reconnaissance of the place, my only visit to 'the Rock'. Likewise to Malta, but we were not allowed ashore. Life was fun and games aboard *Stratheden* – lots of laughs with a group of ENSA entertainers, some of whom hit the big-time post-war.

We disembarked at Alexandria, and *Stratheden* did a quick turn round to take troops home and no doubt, bring some more back. In the company of my very good friend, Dr. Jocelyn Reynolds RNVR, I caught a train to Cairo. We visited the pyramids with our two particular ENSA actresses and also explored Cairo. In Cairo, I met Harry McGowan who was on the Staff of the Eighth Army in Cairo. His brother Billy was very badly shot up in his tank in the Desert, but his life was saved by his father, who had become Lord McGowan, the boss of ICI, getting Penicillin to him just in time. Penicillin, although discovered by a Scotsman, Alexander Fleming, was being marketed for the first time by an American Drug Company, so Harry Senior was able to procure it. Harry Senior was the same one who pulled strings for me to get into the Navy in 1940. Harry Junior gave Jos Reynolds and myself a great evening in the famous Gezira Club.

A day at the Pyramids
en route to Colombo ~ 1944

One day, I went to the British Military Hospital in Heliopolis to look for some friends. There, to my astonishment, I found Dennis Williams who had been blown up in his destroyer, *HMS Hurworth*, in the Aegean Sea and was missing, believed killed. He had already survived *HMS Worcester's* terrible damage in the battle with the *Scharnhorst* and company earlier. I was able to tell Dennis's parents that I took back my glowing obituary letter that I had sent them.

After passing through the Suez Canal, I cannot remember how, Jos and I embarked on *HMS Rocket*, a modern, very much larger destroyer than the Hunts. We had a lovely untroubled cruise across the Indian Ocean in *Rocket*, under the command of Lieutenant Commander Ackroyd. We were treated as honoured guests and had no work to do, as the ship already carried her own doctor.

HMS Bherunda

We eventually sailed into Colombo Harbour in Ceylon and were then quartered in *HMS Bherunda* that had formerly been Colombo Racecourse. The runway straddled the middle of the racetrack. I joined *Bherunda* in February 1944 and left in October 1944. *Bherunda* was a Fleet Air Arm Shore Base and was very busy with training aircrews in Barracuda and Avenger torpedo bombers and Hellcat and Corsair fighters. There were also communication flights between the several naval establishments in Ceylon, and of course, Trincomalee, on the east coast of Ceylon, a vast natural harbour that was home to our Eastern Fleet.

Whilst in Colombo, we had a great life and made many friends of both sexes. Travel around Colombo was by hand-pulled rickshaw. We swam, we golfed and we went to many parties in what was probably the prototype of the Garden of Eden.

Life in *HMS Bherunda* was great. As regards work, we were supernumerary to the establishment, but, as Tropical Medicine and Hygiene experts and in view of our impending dispersal to places near and far, we had a lot to do getting our teams together, ready for what came next. Jos Reynolds went to the Cocos and Keeling Islands where he did great work. My parting 'Flimsy' from the Commanding Officer *Bherunda* was – "satisfactory but takes ill to discipline."

I went off to Southern India with the Fleet Air Arm squadrons for them to do further flying training. We re-opened a disused RAF station near Trichinopoly called Ulunderpet, arriving there on 14 April 1944.

Ulunderpet

*M*y notebook, which I discovered in my tin trunk that had lain in Bentfield attic untouched for many years, disclosed when I opened it, a lot of memorabilia both from my medical student days and wartime exploits. Notes written whilst at Ulunderpet revealed details of the Fleet Air Arm Squadrons. They were 815, 817, 822 and 823 Torpedo Aircraft of the 12th and 45th Wing, as well as 1839 and 1844 fighter aircraft of the 5th Fighter Wing.

The Commanding Officers were Lt. Cdrs. Lawson, May, Brittan, Douglas, Jeram, and finally, Lt. Cdr. Tommy Harrington whom I met years later when he was in the Pharmaceutical Company, Smith Kline and French.

The accommodation in Ulunderpet was in wattle or *kadgan* huts. The place had been abandoned except for caretakers who formed a RAF skeleton staff. One RAF Officer there proudly told me that he was shot down whilst in Coastal Command, which was reported as one of the RAF's 'first kills' of the war – true or false, I wonder?

I was, of course, Wine Caterer. My method was to charge 10 rupees for every drink, so I stuffed my suitcase with ten rupee notes. When it was full and our stocks of wine were getting low, I set off for Trichinopoly to get more gin at Parry's Distillery. On these trips, I drove a 15 cwt. truck, as the young pilots had mostly not learned to drive anything but an aeroplane!

We had a leave rota from Ulunderpet to Colombo and I always made sure that we had a cask of Parry's Gin aboard our aeroplane, which of course was declared 'Duty Free' on arrival.

I made as many sorties as I could and had wonderful holidays in the Ceylon Hill Country around Kandy and Nuwara Eliya whilst on leave.

Many years later, whilst on holiday with Aileen and Bruce in the Hill Club in Nuwara Eliya, I met an old servant, complete with his tortoiseshell comb who said, "Good to see you Master, things are very different now!"

On the sad side, we lost quite a few young pilots during this training period both in India and Ceylon. I remember seeing a huge hole in the ground where the only recognisable human remains was a thumb. The squadrons were eventually ordered to join the Fleet Carrier *HMS Indomitable*, so the planes were flown on to the flight decks somewhere at sea.

HMS Indomitable

HMS INDOMITABLE

I joined my friends of the Squadron on board *Indomitable*, now based in Trincomalee. We did lots of training flights and on several occasions, had our aircraft bombing the Andaman Islands that were Japanese occupied.

Trincomalee was a most beautiful place. I had several friends in the Navy ashore of both sexes, and went for long cycle rides into the jungle. I recall having an 'RPC' – in Naval parlance, Request the Pleasure of Company – to go on board *Illustrious*, our sister ship. On board this ship, a young officer said, "Terribly sorry to hear about your father." That was a shock! I knew he had been ill, but I did not know he had died.

In these operations against the Andamans, and I think the Nicobars as well, we had no retaliation from the Japs for some reason. However, we lost a few pilots when our Barracudas failed to gain enough height on take off, being over-laden with torpedoes and being underpowered with their single engines.

One memorable occasion on *Indomitable* was a 'Crossing the Line' ceremony – i.e. The Equator. There was a party on the flight deck at King Neptune's Court, complete with King Neptune's barber shaving off some senior officer's beard! I remember accepting a dare to jump off the flight deck into the water and, with some shipmates, we dropped into the Indian Ocean. It seemed a long way down, but we were promptly picked up and hauled back on board!

The *Indomitable* was sent for a refit in Bombay and the Squadrons were again back in Ceylon, getting ready for the final assault on the Japanese in Malaya and Singapore. A huge build-up of ships and men was being planned. I left *Indomitable* and the Squadrons, but before doing so, I had occasion to voice an opinion that many of the young pilots were very stressed. The expression then was 'twitch'. My observations were dismissed at first, but a great man, Captain Bill Sears R.N. of vast Fleet Air Arm experience and battles, took me seriously. So, with his help and encouragement, I arranged for Rest and Recreation in a famous Leave Camp, Ootacamund.

Ootacamund

I flew to Bangalore in a Stinson Reliant, a high wing single engine monoplane of the Communication Flight – just two of us, the pilot and myself. He suddenly let go the controls and said, "You drive for a while Doc, I want to sleep". So we changed places. I was told to climb sufficiently high to miss the Nilgiri Mountains. I soon got the hang of the joystick and cleared the mountains with about 2000ft. to spare!

Our navigation on that trip was mainly by low flying and looking at road signposts!

I made contact with the 'powers that be' in Ootacamund and a rota was started to give groups of pilots and navigators a well-earned rest and recreation period in such lovely surroundings. Whilst in Ooty, I dropped into a café and saw the sign about the door 'Arran View'. There, to my great pleasure, I met my cousin Billy Breckenridge of Kilwinning Road, Irvine on leave from the Burma Jungle.

Billy Breckenridge and Percy Walker
Ootacamund ~ 1944

The Irvine, Ayrshire Battery of Gunners, was a family affair. Brigadier General James W. Walker, CMG, DSO, was their C.O. in the First World War. My other uncles in Kilwinning Road, Irvine, were all gunners together in 1914-18. In the second time round, their sons, cousins and friends, kept up the Artillery tradition and spent their war in the Burma jungle. Cousin Willie Breckenridge, Captain Royal Artillery and Lieutenant Gordon Watson, Royal Artillery, both of Kilwinning Road, were killed in Burma, as was Murray Wilson from Kilwinning Road, paradoxically not by the Japanese but by a premature burst whilst firing their artillery piece.

On return to Colombo, our Squadrons had disappeared to some other airfield, Katakurunda in Ceylon, I think. I received yet another draft chit to proceed to *HMS Braganza*, the huge naval establishment in Bombay.

Having left *Indomitable*, I must say that I again was lucky. The *Indomitable* saw a tremendous lot of action against the Japs, both before and after I was on board. My last time on board was when *Indomitable* anchored off Ayr Harbour in the 1950s. She sent a signal for any ex-naval personnel in the district to come on board for drinks. So, I was very delighted to get back on board my old ship, and had a good look round – of course, all the faces were different. *Indomitable* met her end in the breakers yard in Cairnryan down in Wigtownshire.

HMS Braganza

I arrived onboard *HMS Braganza* in Bombay on 17 October 1944 and remained there until 13 August 1945. *Braganza* was a naval base shared with the Royal Indian Navy. Most of us lived in accommodation in the city. I was lucky enough to be given a very nice 'cabin' in a flat called *Firdaus* in Marina Drive, facing the sea. I had very few duties except for sometimes relieving the establishment doctors by taking a sick parade. *Firdaus* had been taken over as a Naval Officers' Headquarters.

Firdaus ~ Naval Officers' Quarters
Marine Drive, Bombay – Aileen at front door (Round the World 1979)

I played golf at the Bombay Willingdon Club, swam at Juhu Beach and, as far as my budget allowed, enjoyed myself in Bombay's nightlife. I was severely restricted in pleasure activities, as I was still having part of my pay deducted due to the Lofoten Islands allotment business. My good friends, Surgeon Lieutenant John Bolton Carter and Surgeon Lieutenant J. D. Watson, with whom I spent most of my leisure life, were not only on full pay, but were receiving an extra 'shore allowance' for which, for some reason, I did not qualify.

Surgeon Lt. (D) Aileen Gerrard Digby RNVR

*O*ne day, I heard that a troopship was arriving in Bombay, so I went down to the Docks.   As this mighty P&O Liner *Strathmore* was disembarking its passengers, I spotted a lovely lady in her white naval uniform.   She was not a Wren, but a Naval Lieutenant with an orange stripe between her two gold braid stripes – a 'Toothwright!'   I think I managed to get near her, but she was surrounded by a bodyguard of young officers who had been vying for her attention whilst on passage from Liverpool.

Surgeon Lieutenant (D) Aileen Gerrard Digby was the lady in question.   A typical Irish beauty from Dublin, with jet black hair, Irish eyes and a figure that would take your breath away.

Aileen Digby ~ aged about two, with her Mother

Aileen had joined the Navy like so many thousands of people from the Irish Republic. She joined the British Forces in spite of their Country's nominal neutrality.

Her first 'ship' was a Wireless and Signals training station at a Holiday Camp in Ayr, my home County of course. An officer there, a seventh son of a seventh son, prophesied that she would eventually return to Scotland. She was on a train from Ayr to Glasgow one day, en route to Liverpool to take passage to India, when she got into conversation with a lady who said that she had some of her own family and relations in far off places and a nephew, a doctor in the Navy, in the Far East. Aileen was particularly struck by this lady who, unknown to Aileen, was the wife of Brigadier General James Walker, my uncle. She remembered this lady's Artillery diamond brooch.

Surgeon Lt. (D) Aileen Digby RNVR
whilst in HM Scotia AYR (before the fortune teller's words came true)

My luck continued! Aileen was sent to the Naval Officers' accommodation in *Firdaus*, previously mentioned, where I had a 'cabin' on the floor below the Wrens' flat.

Not unnaturally, being the first female Naval dentist to go overseas, Aileen was in great demand. Senior Officers and lesser fry were vying for a chance to take her out. I could not compete with them, because I could barely afford to take myself out (allotment trouble). One evening, she turned up, escorted by a very Senior Officer. She was dressed in her 'Number Tens', an evening rig for Officers in tropical stations – white tunic buttoned up to the neck. "Good God, woman, take that off, you are east of Suez now, put on a dress" was the order! I consoled myself by getting a glimpse of Aileen on the stairs of *Firdaus* on her way back from her nightly 'runs ashore'. I played my cards as well as I could. I was **MADLY** in love with her.

Aileen on the roof of Firdaus

It was certainly my first experience of this phenomenon, in spite of many happy female friendships. I never lacked self-confidence, but I was never strong on self-esteem in relation to my ability to impress the ladies. I now think that this is a characteristic which can appeal to the ladies, although not if it is a deliberate ploy. To my delight and astonishment, Aileen seemed to think that I was 'no bad' as we say in Scotland.

I suppose that it was a conditioned reflex in a way, but I developed severe toothache. Aileen diagnosed it as an un-erupted wisdom tooth and made arrangements to remove it herself.

Her Senior Surgeon Commander (D) was not entirely in favour of her tackling such a complicated job, but she persevered and eventually I was admitted to a Bombay Hospital where the deed was successfully performed. I had been given a general anaes-thetic for the job and, on coming round, I had, while still semi-conscious, a terrible premonition that something was wrong with Aileen. Against the advice and protestations of the Indian nurses, I escaped from my bed wearing what I stood up in and ran to *Firdaus*. I remember Surgeon Commander Besley R.N., Senior Medical Officer of *Braganza* being astonished at me appearing in the Officer's Mess at drinks time in my shorts and my face still swollen. So, although he must have felt the need to reprimand me, he was very gentle and told me to go to my cabin. There he told me that Aileen had been admitted to another hospital in Bombay with a very sudden and severe dose of typhoid fever. She had always loved oysters and had devoured them the night before at a 'Taj Mahal' party, unaware, of course, of their contamination with the Typhoid Bacillus. Luckily, she had had her inoculations, or my story might have been very different from this point.

I shall never forget the torment of these few weeks. Aileen's life was in the balance for three or so weeks and to complicate matters, the socket from which my tooth had been extracted became septic, not uncommon in hot climates. I was in agony with a very swollen face and could not eat, just able to drink. I spent endless hours in my cabin, sometimes ringing the hospital not being able to bear waiting for the phone to ring me. I knew that she had been anointed with 'the last rites' of the Catholic Church.

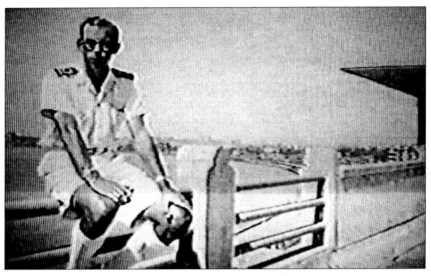

Percy on the roof of Firdaus

Aileen on Juhu Beach with Fortune Teller

Our Engagement

A former Destroyer doctor and colleague, now Surgeon Lt. Commander Dai Pugh, D.S.C., RNVR, was the physician in charge of the Naval Wing of the Bombay Hospital where Aileen was lying. He also had his Fellowship of the Royal College of Physicians and he was in charge of Aileen's ward. Aileen and I both owe a tremendous amount to Dai's skill and optimism, although when Aileen was still delirious, I spotted an entry in her case sheet taking up the whole page: "This poor woman has delusions, she thinks that she is engaged to Percy Walker." Surgeon Commander Besley ordered me to remain at Aileen's bedside day and night – more or less. Not a problem for me! Like everyone else, Commander Besley was very fond of Aileen and must have already spotted our 'relationship' – not so strong a word then as it is now!

My sore mouth soon recovered and I remember vividly sitting at Aileen's bedside. She would lapse in and out of consciousness. Once, a serene smile came on her face and I thought she was slipping away. Much later, we heard from Aileen's mother that at that very moment, she, i.e. Aileen's mother, woke up in Dublin (we checked the date and time later) shouting, "Aileen, Aileen, oh God, please save her!" I remember waking Aileen from her dream, which would almost certainly have been her last. I can't remember what I said, but she opened her eyes and smiled at ME. She told me later that she was slipping down a long tunnel with a light at the end.

That was the turning point, but she was still in a semi-typhoid coma.

One day, however, she said, "We are engaged aren't we?" My heart leapt and I said, "YES, WE ARE." I took off my signet ring and put in on her finger. She gradually picked up strength and showed off the ring to the nurses. But, soon, she fully regained her senses. She had no recollection whatsoever of the circumstances surrounding the engagement!

However, I was so thrilled to be engaged that I sent notices to the Glasgow Herald and the Irish Times and, of course, sent a telegram to Aileen's parents in Dublin. Two telegrams arrived within a short time of each other. The first one, "We regret to inform you." The telephonist in Dublin prefixed her message by saying, "It's not as bad as it sounds." What a relief but what a fright and what a nice telephonist! Shortly after this telegram, another one arrived in Dublin from ME, requesting Mr. and Mrs. Digby's permission to take Aileen's hand in marriage. Poor souls, one can only imagine their confusion. Aileen did remember events leading up to her sudden and profound attack of typhoid but, as I said, had no recollection of the 'engagement'. However, I honourably indicated that I would bide my time and not push the matter, and in a very short time, we both reverted to the situation pre-typhoid except that we were now really engaged, I insisted!

Commander Besley sent us both on leave, Aileen on sick leave and myself on compassionate, or should I say 'passionate', leave. Aileen was still skeletal and very weak on the legs. We had a lovely time up in the hill country where the British Raj would formerly escape from the heat of the plains, in Dehra Dun and then Mussoorie. We rode on horses and walked when Aileen gradually became stronger and stronger. Whilst in Mussoorie, the war in Europe came to an end – unconditional surrender by the Germans and the end of Hitler and his Nazis. Both Hitler and Mussolini died in the manner in which millions of innocents had died – brutally. We heard of the V.E. celebrations whilst in Mussoorie. In spite of the ecstatic elation, we realised that we still had the Japs to deal with.

Dehra Dun ~ 1944
"Watch your Saluting"

"Baksheez Memsahib" ~ 1944
Aileen with friends - Marbaleshwar

I bought Aileen what I thought was a proper engagement ring, but I was seen off by the jeweller. The 'diamonds' were 'paste'. I did later give her another really genuine ring, which still adorns her finger.

On return to Bombay, in the Frontier Mail Express of the Bombay and Central India Railway, Aileen was given a 'medical' and was then to be repatriated to the U.K. I was to be part of an Allied force assembling to sail across to Malaya and Singapore, to send the Japs back where they came from. Aileen returned to Britain on another P&O Liner, was it the *Strathmore* or the *Strathnaver*? After a spell of sick leave at home, she was drafted to the Royal Naval Barracks, *HMS Drake*, in Devonport. Her accommodation was in a Nissen-hutted, Wrens quarters in Plymouth.

By all accounts, both at the time and later, Aileen had a great time in Devonport, but never forgot that she was engaged, even if she did not always display the ring.

I shared a cabin, still in Firdaus, with Lieutenant Noble, RN, son of the famous Admiral Noble. He had been the First Lieutenant of *Garth* when I was the M.O. We shared a bearer, Diya, who looked after us well but was a bit light-fingered. I met him in the street one day and recognised him from behind, as he was wearing one of my shirts inside out, with the name 'A.P. Walker' on the collar. In spite of that, I gave him a tremendously good testimonial to give to his next Sahib. One time, this same bearer, Diya, gave me a present of what he called, 'sacred bark'. He said, "Sahib, run this sacred bark on Sahib's forehead when Sahib has too much drink and Sahib will be able to have more drink" – I wish I still had the sacred bark!

En Route to Malaya

*I*n due course, I was sent to a light carrier, manufactured in bits in the USA and carried across the Atlantic, to be assembled for use in the Royal Navy – 'Woolworth Carriers', they were called. We sailed from Bombay in a huge convoy en route for Malaya. Innumerable troop ships were filled to the gunwales. My job, I was told, was to embark in a small craft to be a medical presence during the assault on the beaches.

On the way across, our Carrier developed engine trouble, so we had to be transferred to another similar ship in mid-ocean. I remember seeing my bicycle dangling from a crane during the transfer. A voice boomed from the Bridge: "What the hell is that bicycle doing here, drop it in the drink Chief!"

I rushed up to the Bridge in time to request the Chief Petty Officer to spare my bicycle – I still have it.

Shortly after transferring ships, a voice came over the tannoy, "The Japanese have unconditionally surrendered." Atomic bombs had been dropped by the Allies on two Japanese cities, Hiroshima and Nagasaki. I was lucky yet again, but not so the inhabitants of those two cities. I remember the reaction of the American troops on board our ship in contrast to the British attitude. The American troops shouted and yelled, "God Save America!" But my sick berth attendant whose hammock was slung beside mine, said, "And about ……. time, too!" I went to sleep again.

The Bicycle – I still have it!
Percy and Robert off to golf

Port Swettenham and Singapore

*O*n arrival at Port Swettenham in Malaya, the port for Kuala Lumpur, there was no war to fight. Hard luck on the planners! It was also tough on the thousands of troops, a lot of them Indians and Ghurkas thirsting for Japanese blood! They were closeted in their overcrowded ships and became quite unruly. The Japs had, in fact, left Malaya in a hurry except for a few stragglers who helped? Voluntarily? – I wonder – to disembark men and material.

I got a lift up to Kuala Lumpur, a beautiful city, but probably unrecognisable now: I think that it has the world's highest tower now. I had a look around and then returned to Port Swettenham through huge rubber plantations. It is amazing how so much rubber can be produced from one little container attached to the bark of a rubber tree.

One thing I remember about Port Swettenham was that our troops, or some of them, felt free to commandeer cars and lorries from the native population. I was rather disgusted by this, but on reflection, the previous owners no doubt had their own property commandeered by the Japs.

Things were very disorganised. Nobody seemed to be in charge of me, or seemed to care anyway.

I spotted my old friend *M.V. Sobieski*, the Polish liner, alongside the quay. So, with all my baggage including the bicycle, I walked up the gangplank. The same crew was on board as on my trip to Algiers and back. I received a warm welcome, but these poor, proud Poles were dejected and resentful at how their country had been yet again partitioned. Huge chunks of territory had been lost when Churchill, Roosevelt and Stalin met at Yalta. The massacre of fellow Poles was too ghastly to contemplate. *Sobieski* sailed that night for Singapore.

On arrival there, I installed myself in an Officers' Mess ashore. I was there for a few weeks, long enough to sightsee. It included a trip on my bicycle over the Johore Causeway, which had provided the Japs with easy access to overrun Singapore from the North where they had landed at Kotabahru on the East Coast of Malaya. The guns and defence works of Singapore had all been pointing out to sea, so were not much use!

The horrors of the fall of Singapore and subsequent prison camps are a different story from mine, but I did know that a Captain William Handley Ferguson, Royal Horse Artillery, a Regular Soldier, had been captured by the Japs, and had been reported as a Prisoner of War. So, one day, I cycled to the infamous Changi Jail and found 'Fergie's' name on a list at the gate.

I found his hut. He was barely recognisable. I had met him often in peacetime when he was courting my first cousin Rosalie Cory, daughter of my father's sister, Aunt Bessie. He was sitting at a table with some fellow POWs. They were emaciated, hollow-eyed and gaunt, with swollen bellies and legs, resulting from Beri Beri. Poor Fergie's face lit up when I was able to tell him that Rosalie, his wife, was fit and well, as was his mother-in-law of whom he was very fond. Any news for Fergie from the UK, probably very sparse, would be likely to indicate that Britain was finished – Japanese propaganda no doubt. The POWs had not the strength to open tins of fruit provided by an Australian repatriation organisation called RAPW (Repatriation of Allied Prisoners of War), so I opened the tins, but the contents immediately made them sick – they had not eaten anything but rice for years!

Fergie recovered sufficiently to be sent home. There is a story, no longer contradictable, as Fergie died in the eighties, that before going home, he retrieved all his belongings, mess kit, etc., from the railway station's left luggage office somewhere in the Malaya Peninsula. He had 'left his luggage' in a hurry, when his unit was overwhelmed by Japs. Dawn, his lovely daughter was born post-war, whilst his son Shane was a pre-war baby. Shane sadly died in 2001. Dawn is now a supernumerary daughter, married to our good friend Greville Vernon.

Having seen all I could in Singapore, I was wandering around the docks one day with all my accoutrements of war, in the hope of getting back as soon as I could, when I spotted the Royal Navy Cruiser, *HMS Glasgow*, which appeared to be on the point of departure. I was missing my fiancée dreadfully, and communications were non-existent due to my being of 'no fixed abode'. I quickly ascended the gangplank just before she 'slipped'. A charming First Lieutenant said, "Name please, Doc?" I told him and he said, "I don't seem to have your name on my list." We were only being allowed home according to our demobilisation status. I told him that I was acting under my own orders and he graciously said that every cabin was already full of returning servicemen, but no doubt I would be comfortable in the Admiral's quarters. *Glasgow* was not acting as flagship on that particular voyage, so I had a very pleasant five-star journey from Singapore to Colombo.

I then caught a train to Jaffna, took the ferry across the so-called Abraham's Bridge and sailed to Madras. After a few days there in the Connemara Hotel (quite prophetic), I took a train to somewhere. Bombay was my ultimate destination. By this time, my journey homeward had been more or less regularised and approved. Part of my trip was in a Dakota aircraft with no seats – just packing cases – and I seem to remember breaking my journey in Cochin, still with my bicycle!

Home!

*E*ventually, I reached Bombay and, now being a bona fide traveller, I sailed to Suez. From there, I sailed home in the P&O Liner *Strathnaver*, similar to the *Stratheden*, on which I had sailed from Gourock to Alexandria some years previously. I think Southampton was our port of entry and I made my way to Euston Station where I left all my luggage in an underground cellar, as I said I would not be back for a while and my gear was too voluminous for the ordinary left luggage office. By this time, I had contacted Aileen in Devonport by phone, an exciting moment for both us. The timing was good in that my mother was due to arrive in Shrewsbury for my youngest brother Campbell's Speech Day. This was in June 1945. Aileen travelled up from Plymouth to Shrewsbury to meet us. The train was four hours late and I still remember the wait on Shrewsbury platform. How was it all going to work out? I had no doubts myself! Eventually, she arrived looking terrific, this time in her navy-blue uniform. "No problems!" My mother heartily agreed with my choice and also fell in love with Aileen. Aileen had to return to Plymouth when the weekend was up. I went back to Euston, retrieved my gear and went back to Campbellfield, Irvine. Nothing had changed except it was very strange and sad without my father.

Apparently, when my father was terminally ill, my friend Lieutenant Dennis Williams, DSC, RNVR, whom I met in Heliopolis and who was on sick leave after his experiences in the Aegean, was a tremendous help to my mother.

My second, middle brother, Robert, four years younger than I, took seriously ill during his time on an Officer Training Unit. He had just received a Commission in the Queen's Own Cameron Highlanders and had to be invalided out. However, he was fit for service with the Home Guard at home where he did sterling work. I remember going to see him in hospital near Birmingham, where he looked terribly ill. I think I had leave from the *Southdown* to go and visit him.

Aileen in Navy Blue

My sister Kathleen spent her war as a VAD Nurse in various Coastal Forces Naval Stations and subsequently left nursing to become an Ambulance Driver. Between Kathleen, Robert and Campbell, they gave tremendous support to our mother who was devastated by her husband's death at the early age of 60.

For a while I was in 'limbo', still in uniform, which I wore when I needed such things as petrol coupons and access to many service parties around, but soon my Demobilisation papers arrived. I went to Glasgow to get fitted with my Demob suit – not too bad, but I seldom wore it. I enrolled in a scheme for postgraduate studies for returning Medical Officers in Glasgow. The courses were well intentioned, but very inadequate, but I was paid £350 per annum!

I firstly travelled daily from home to the Western Infirmary, Glasgow, of happy memories, and then to the Royal Infirmary. Being 'attached' to the hurly burly of life in the wards and clinics, without any responsibility, one was actually taught very little in the Surgical Wards of the former, and similarly, when I did an attachment to Medical Wards in the latter.

Wedding Bells

*E*ither during or just after these courses in Glasgow, Aileen and I arranged for our Wedding Bells.

By this time, I had sailed across the Irish Sea to Dublin and was greeted by Aileen's parents, brothers and sister with a very warm welcome, although they must have been somewhat apprehensive. Apart from anything else, I was a Scots Presbyterian, although I had also been confirmed in the Anglican Church at Shrewsbury – and after a few years of marriage, I became a Catholic.

So, a date was fixed for the Wedding, June 20th 1946. We asked a fair number of our friends from Scotland but the journey to Ireland then seemed like a very long one. However, about a dozen or more friends, our contemporaries, made the trip. They went on either The Royal Scotsman or The Royal Ulsterman from the Broomielaw to Belfast. Both of these lovely ships of the Burns Laird Line had just finished their major refit after hectic wartime service.

The wedding party then went by train from Belfast to Dublin. My father-in-law-to-be was a founder member of the Irish Tourist Board newly set up after the war. He installed the guests in the beautiful new Portmarnock Country Club – and paid the bills!

Aileen and I had been married the day before on the 20th June in the Catholic Church in Irvine. Father O'Reilly officiated, Father Murphy, my father's old friend having departed. In spite of all Aileen's and her parent's efforts, the Archbishop of Dublin had made it virtually impossible for a Catholic to marry a non-Catholic in his diocese. So we had a nuptial service in Irvine with Aileen's brother Dillon, sister Patricia, my family and some cousins present.

MARRIAGES

WALKER and DIGBY—June 20, 1946, at St. Mary's, Irvine, Ayrshire, Dr. A. Percy Walker, eldest son of the late T. C. Walker and Mrs. Walker, Campbellfield, Irvine, to Aileen, elder daughter of Mr. and Mrs. J. P. Digby, Mill House, Dundrum, Co. Dublin.

In common with tradition, as Aileen was staying in Campbellfield, I spent the pre-wedding night across the road with my Breckenridge cousins. We had a small celebration at Campbellfield afterwards, then wedding guests went from Glasgow to Belfast and on to Dublin. The newly weds themselves caught the Glasgow-Stranraer Boat Express which made a special stop at Irvine for us; I am not quite sure how I managed that!

We sailed from Stranraer to Larne on the *Princess Margaret*, a rather clapped out, old, coal-burning vessel that was very war weary. Being newly weds, I at least, did not mind being kept awake all night by coal being loaded right above our cabin. The bunk was not designed for two people, but that also was OK by me!

We arrived at Dublin by train from Belfast, a different train from the guests, and were whisked off to join both Irish and Scottish guests at a nuptial banquet in Portmarnock, the likes of which the Scots had not seen during years of war.

Wedding Group
Mill House Dundrum, Dublin ~ June 1946

The Irish hospitality was fabulous and unforgettable. The following day, the Reception took place in the lovely garden of Mill House, Dundrum, County Dublin, the home of Aileen's parents, Mr. and Mrs. J. P. Digby. I recall beautiful weather, too. It was a lavish affair, food and drink unending. The Digby Black Labrador, Barry, buried a bottle of champagne for his future use in his outdoor kennel.

Wedding Reception ~ Mill House 1946

After the Reception, the guests went back to the Portmarnock Country Club for another orgy.

In accordance with ancient tradition, now thank goodness no longer, the newly weds did not go to the party – we went elsewhere south of Dublin for the night. By this time, my mother's little Morris had arrived by cargo vessel in Dublin Harbour, so we were able to drive off by ourselves.

Our next port of call was to spend a week in the most luxurious place imaginable, Ashford Castle, Cong, in the West of Ireland beside the famous Lough Corrib, the largest freshwater lake in the Republic. To say that it was an idyllic honeymoon would be an understatement.

"Our Honeymoon Hideaway"
Ashford Castle, Cong, Ireland

Knowing each other physically, as well as mentally, was an ecstatic experience – we were both novices! In Aileen's case, an Irish Convent School had without doubt instilled the importance of morality. In my case, I remember when I was about 10 years old, our family doctor had said to my father, "Tom! I think it's about time you told that boy about the facts of life." So, one night, my mother was sent to the spare bedroom whilst I moved into her bed. My father must have been nervous about telling me too much, or too little, so he settled for, "Keep away from dirty women." In later life, no matter what the temptation, I remembered his words regardless of the hygienic status of the lady in question – who could be certain anyway?

So, I have come to the conclusion that ignorance and fear might well be a better inhibitor than the explicit sex education of today. I wonder if the present day young are not missing out when premarital intimacy now seems to be the norm? I am sure that the commitment of marriage ensures a much more stable relationship in spite of the inevitable ups and downs. Nowadays, a honeymoon must be just another holiday. I could be old fashioned and ignorant of the present situation, but, like swans; I am in favour of a mate for life.

After a week at Ashford, we moved further West into the heart of Connemara, another unbelievably beautiful place – Ballynahinch Castle. This beautiful place was formerly home to Rangit Singhi, an Indian Prince of unlimited wealth. The house sits on the side of Ballynahinch River, looking down from a height to the river below. The river is one of Ireland's many and famous salmon rivers. We remember huge gourmet meals prepared by a top French Chef brought to launch this new hotel as the flagship of the Irish Tourist Board. The place lived up to expectations! We explored the lovely countryside, some wooded and some wildly desolate, wherein lay its beauty. Oliver Cromwell was said to have dispatched his enemies to 'Hell or Connaught'.

Ballynahinch Castle, County Galway
Our next honeymoon hideaway

Aileen on one of Twelve Pins
Honeymoon ~ Connemara 1946

The whole countryside now attracts a huge number of tourists and, resulting from Irish affluence since joining the European Union, has thousands of second homes scattered over the countryside. Too many people seem to be seeking solitude. The only thing that slightly clouded my immense enjoyment of these lovely places, was, "What are my future prospects as a doctor?"

Aileen had to return to *HMS* Drake in Devonport to go through the demobilisation process. To her eternal credit, she turned down promotion to Lieutenant Commander (D) in favour of leaving the Navy to become a dutiful wife. I wonder how I would have fared with a wife being my Senior Officer?

Rothesay

I was, naturally, hard up, having been paid off and having no job. I was lucky to get a job as a 'locum tenens' in a General Practice in Rothesay, capital of the beautiful Isle of Bute. A friend, Willie Greig, who ran a pharmaceutical company, found me the job. So, I sailed to Rothesay and was met by Mrs. Christie, 1 Battery Place, Rothesay, situated beside the pier. Her husband, Dr. Christie, had literally burnt himself out as a single handed General Practitioner during the War. So, when I got to Rothesay, Dr. Christie had already had a coronary and was in hospital on the mainland. Mrs. Christie was a very formidable lady – a pillar of temperance, she made it very clear about what I was to do and was not to do.

A cavalcade of steamers arrived at Rothesay every morning – *Queen Mary II* from Gourock to Ardrishaig (the Macbrayne Mail Boat for Kintyre), the LNER *Marmion* from Craigendoran, followed by the former Williamson Buchanan Line, either *King Edward* or *Queen Alexandria*, and then the Caledonian Steam Packet, *Duchess of Montrose*, cruising from Gourock to Dunoon, Rothesay, Kyles of Bute and Lochranza. The *Jeannie Deans* and *Waverley* from Craigendoran also passed through Rothesay.

Mrs. Christie was very determined that anyone off the boat should be inveigled into 1 Battery Place rather than to her husband's rival GPs down the road. I felt woefully inadequate as a doctor. I was still suffering from deliberately avoiding postgraduate work after qualifying, resulting from jumping the queue to get into the Navy.

The refresher courses immediately after demobilisation were really window dressing. I do not blame anyone for this, as the hospital staffs were tired, war weary and not geared to teaching returning medical officers from the Services. It really was a great strain trying to do one's best for patients, with so little idea how to do so. The National Health Service was still a long way off dream.

I erred on the side of safety by prescribing medicines that were fairly harmless, whilst at the same time trying to exude much more confidence than I possessed. The patients at least did not seem to get any worse with this very conservative treatment!

My abiding memory of pre-NHS general practice was the inability of so many people to obtain medical help due to abject poverty.

My salary for the month of August 1945 was £60.0s.0d. all in, but meals provided. I had my own car, but I was given a petrol allowance. Mrs. Christie would go through the daily list of patients seen either at the Surgery or on my visits. Every day I was short of takings and had to make it up out of my own pocket. I found it impossible to ask for money from a young mother dying in agony from cancer – a case I shall never forget. She had reached a terminal state before sending for the doctor, because she could not afford to. This observation is certainly not a slight on the country's General Practitioners in general, who were able to charge the 'well-to-do' enough to treat the very poor for little or nothing.

Paradoxically, I often heard in later life the 'well-to-do' expressing the wish to get back to the good old days when you paid your doctor for the service you wanted. Not good old days for the not so well off.

I muddled through my month in Rothesay. Halfway through my time there, I heard from Aileen in Plymouth that she was about to be demobbed. I was over the moon at this news, but as I had the job as a 'single man', Mrs. Christie did not take kindly to the locum having a woman in his bedroom.

However, I suppose I was indispensable under the circumstances, I say modestly. So, it was arranged that the doctor and his wife were to be installed in a guesthouse on the outskirts of Rothesay, the Craignethan Private Hotel. I met Aileen on the mainland and sailed back to Rothesay with her.

I was working all day and a lot of the night for the whole month. There was no arrangement for half days off with the other GPs, so Aileen had a fairly quiet time of it for the remaining fortnight of my contract.

We did, however, manage to explore the beautiful Island of Bute where my maternal grandmother, Mary Jane Kerr Macalister, eventually Reid, had been brought up in Mid Ascog Farm.

We also took a short cruise on one of the Clyde Steamers to the Cowal Games in Dunoon. Mrs. Christie must have been in a good mood that day. She had a horror of the evils of drink, which resulted in a complete intolerance even of my very moderate indulgence. One weekend, her son came home to visit her. He suggested that I might like to join him for a drink in a nearby pub. I accepted with alacrity. What we did not realise was that Mother had us in view through her binoculars. I would not have got off so lightly if Master Christie had not been my companion!

At last the month was over – a great relief to me and no doubt to my patients. Poor Doctor Christie died shortly after my time in his practice, where by all accounts, he had been a wonderfully kind and good doctor.

Samaritan Hospital

*A*ileen and I took up our residence in Campbellfield. We were still 'broke', so Aileen managed to get a job with the County Council School Dental Service. I was yet again wondering which way my medical career would take me. Everyone said, "I presume you are going to specialise?" So, I got a live-in job at the Samaritan Hospital in Glasgow, purpose-built for gynaecology. Once more, Post Graduate ex-Service doctors were supernumerary to the day-to-day activities at the hospital. My mate was a South African doctor called Heyman Isodore Schmulze, a most likeable and amusing colleague who had qualified at the University of Witwatersrand, and hoped to get valuable experience in Glasgow.

Mr. Donald McIntyre was in charge of our hospital unit. Definitely one of the 'old school', he was always immaculately dressed, drove in a *Rolls Royce* with a chauffeur, had a large private practice and got through his hospital work efficiently and diligently. He did, however, treat his private patients as a different species to the poor, not in the medical sense of treatment, but as regards to communication and respect.

Schmulze and I were, at best, spectators of the goings on in the hospital. Halfway through our six months attachment, Schmulze and I plotted to bring our disquiet and dissatisfaction to the attention of the great Mr. McIntyre. He always arrived at the hospital on time to the minute. I took his coat and hung it up and Schmulze took his hat and cane – for three months. One day, Mr. McIntyre was met by two angry rebels. To his total astonishment, we threw his coat, hat and stick to the ground. He listened to our complaint with fairly kindly tolerance, considering our unquestionable rudeness. He turned to Sister Suttie, a very formidable lady and said, "Sister, Dr. Schmulze will do the Hysterectomy and Dr. Walker will do the Pelvic Floor repair. I shall assist." The other younger gynaecologists on the staff thought that this was the funniest thing they had ever seen. We had made our point, however, and were much better treated thereafter, and took his coat, hat and stick with good grace.

During this time in the Samaritan, I was still agonising about my future medical career. I was trying to get my Book together for submission to The Royal College of Obstetricians and Gynae-cologists as a preliminary to sitting their Examination for Membership (M.R.C.O.G). Aileen frequently drove up from Irvine to Glasgow in the evening, and appreciated my dilemma. We both decided that carrying on in the Samaritan was getting me nowhere.

Ayrshire Central Maternity Hospital

My luck yet again! Ayrshire Central Maternity Hospital was just outside Irvine, along Kilwinning Road. There I met Richard de Soldenhoff, FRCS, FRCOG, who had just taken over the top job in the hospital from Dr. W.I.C. Morris, a pioneer of modern midwifery. Richard de Soldenhoff, an Edinburgh Graduate of White Russian descent, had had amazing and brilliant highly traumatic experiences as Colonial Service Medical Officer in the infamous railway, Burma-Thailand (the 'Bridge over the River Kwai' line).

Richard and his charming wife, Mollie lived in one of the hospital houses. We became good friends and I managed to get a job as one of his House Surgeons. What a contrast to the 'courses' in the Glasgow hospitals. It was a really hands-on job. We were given maximum responsibility, albeit under scrutiny. Mothers poured in night and day from all over the County of Ayrshire, often in a very poor state, as antenatal care was only just becoming available. We did innumerable deliveries round the clock and never had an uninterrupted night's sleep for three days on end – virtually on duty 24 hours a day for the three days, followed by a blissful night off.

Complicated cases on The District were commonplace, almost a daily occurrence, when the rota demanded our accompanying the Duty Registrar, or more often, the Chief himself, on errands of mercy for difficult labours or Eclampsia cases throughout the County.

It was tremendous experience and invaluable in general practice later, although fortunately, due to infinitely better antenatal care, such emergencies became almost a rarity.

116

Aileen at Hospital Dance with Richard de Soldenhoff

During my time at the Ayrshire Central Hospital, I tried my luck with the Royal College of Obstetricians and Gynaecologists. I travelled to London, went to the Royal Free Hospital for the practical exam and to the College itself for the written exam. I passed! After the examination, before getting the Sleeper back to Kilmarnock, I dropped in to the Brevet Flying Club somewhere in London's West End, and to my delight and astonishment, I met quite a few old mates from the Fleet Air Arm Squadrons. I don't remember the journey home!

Dr. de Soldenhoff offered me a further job as his full time Ante-natal Doctor that entailed travelling to Clinics all over Ayrshire.

During this time, Aileen and I felt that we would love to be on our own. We were lucky enough to find lodgings in a lovely secluded house occupied by a fine old lady, Mrs. (Granny) Sinclair and her daughter and grandchildren. We had a nice sitting room, bedroom and a tiny kitchen. We really enjoyed life in this lovely woodland home, the former Factor's house in Eglinton Estate.

When my job terminated with the Ante Natal Clinics, I managed to get a job with Doctors Gibson and Taylor in an old established General Practice in Irvine. Although an experienced Obstetrician, I still sadly lacked knowledge and experience in general medicine and surgery. So, as in Rothesay, a lot of my treatments were more good luck than good management. However, I hope I did not do anyone more harm than good.

I shall never forget the sheer endless slog of that job both night and day. Dr. Gibson, a wonderful man who had been top brass in the RAMC in the Great War, was dying. Dr. Taylor 'enjoyed' bad health and also enjoyed a refreshment or two. My workmate, a really nice chap called Tom Leven, had been unfit for Military Service. He was a good doctor, but suffered from depression and took solace in drugs. When Dr. Gibson died, after a few months in the job, I was told cursorily by Dr. Taylor that my services were no longer required.

After a few weeks signing on 'the dole', I was again rescued by Richard de Soldenhoff who managed to get me combined appointments as his House Surgeon in Gynaecology and a Surgical Housemanship with Mr. Arthur (Paddy) Sangster and Mr. Gavin Cleland, all in the Ballochmyle Hospital, Mauchline. These latter two doctors were inspiring mentors. They also communicated with their patients, which, sadly, too often seems to be a lost art nowadays.

I was overworked like all junior doctors, but obtained wonderful experience in this former Emergency Medical hospital in a lovely country setting.

Bruce Digby Jude Walker

Not surprisingly, Aileen became pregnant and on 23 November 1947, our son and heir, Bruce Digby Jude Walker was born.

Richard de Soldenhoff looked after Aileen during her pregnancy, which was just as well, because near her time, her blood pressure shot up (pre-Eclampsia) and an emergency Caesarean Section had to be performed. Touch and go for Bruce, hence 'Jude' being in his name – Blessed Saint Jude being the Saint of Hopeless Cases and Matters despaired of.

A Job in Ayr!

*W*hilst attending a British Medical Association Meeting one evening – always on a Sunday then, a former fellow student and also ex-RNVR friend, Archibald MacDonald, approached me. The NHS had started on the 4th July 1948. Most doctors, especially the Establishment, were dead against the NHS, but Aneurin Bevan bribed them by saying he would fill their pockets with gold.

Archie, a Highlander from Arisaig, had joined a very old and beloved General Practitioner in Ayr (then 93 years old) just after the inception of the NHS. Dr. Alexander (Sandy) White was a legend. Poor Sandy White went to his grave wondering why Archie did not pay him a large sum for 'goodwill' – little realising that Aneurin Bevan had abolished 'goodwill' on 4th July 1948.

On the Sunday evening in question, Archie showed me a cheque for over £1,000. He was in good fettle and I suggested he might need a Partner. He seemed to think that this would be a good idea and I was thrilled at the prospect.

I remember not long before, being in despair about my medical future and looking down on the fair town of Ayr, my calf country, from the Heads of Ayr. I prayed there and then that somewhere, somehow, sometime I might get a job in Ayr. The odds against obtaining a post through the 'clearing houses' in a salubrious area were stacked high against me – 200 doctors looking for one job. However, Archie's offer stood, for he remembered our conversation sufficiently to get in touch with a firm of Lawyers in Glasgow who specialised in Medical Partnerships – Crawford, Herron and Cameron. Archie was advised in no uncertain manner that there was no room for two of us in the practice – due to insufficient patients.

I had previously approached a senior GP in Ayr, Dr. Alex Scott, who was Chairman of the newly formed local Medical Committee, and I had also spoken to a great friend of my father, Mr. Walter Galbraith, Chairman of the new Western Regional Hospital Board. Both welcomed me to the fold. So one evening, perhaps because neither Archie nor I were entirely sober under the strain of events, we had a verbal battle. I said, "If one of has to go, it won't be me." Things were getting ugly, when in walked, or staggered, Mrs. Morgan, Archie's housekeeper – he was a bachelor. Mrs. Morgan was a very fun loving young lady who, in spite of a very strict puritanical upbringing, enjoyed life to the full. Archie and I were getting more and more antagonistic when the lady fell on top of us saying, "Boys! Never drink Gordon's Gin," and passed out.

This incident took the heat out of our disagreement. It was the only disagreement we ever had in 30 years together. Soon, we sorted things out, and in spite of Crawford, Herron and Cameron's advice, and in desperation, I agreed to do more or less the bulk of the work for half the pay. So, Archie did the afternoon Surgery from his own house, 25 Prestwick Road, Ayr, taking Friday afternoon and all weekends off, whilst I did morning Surgery, Monday to Saturday in a Chemist's shop in Main Street, Ayr. Robert Bell MPS became a great friend and he knew all the patients and what bottle to give them. I had a table, chair, cold-water sink and a Bunsen burner as equipment. The patient's chair folded flat for further, fuller examination. Except Thursdays, my half-day, I also did all the evening surgeries 6 – 8, including Saturday and Sunday afternoons.

By now, thanks to my time in the Central Hospital (Midwifery) and Ballochmyle (Surgery), I was infinitely better equipped as a doctor. I still suffered severely, however, from a total absence of medical recording in the Practice, so, as often as not, I did not know who was sitting in front of me, or have the faintest idea of what diagnosis if any was attached to the patient, or what treatment they were getting!

The Walker Girls and 107/109 New Road, Ayr

$\mathcal{T}$o digress a little – to our great joy, Patricia Jane Walker arrived on 21st October 1949. She was born under the care of Richard de Soldenhoff, again in Irvine Central, but this time, no Caesarean Section was needed.

I had been living in a totally unfurnished, uncarpeted upper room in Archie's house all this time. My furniture was the camping equipment that I had been allowed to keep after my time with the Royal Marines. Our wedding presents were also stored in the room. Aileen and the babies lived with my mother in Rowantree Cottage in Troon. We had acquired a new Ford Popular – more string pulling in Ireland via a friend of J.P. Digby. New cars were normally impossible to buy then unless one paid hugely over the odds.

My life was really tough then, I was working night and day – with hardly ever an uninterrupted night's sleep. Part of the agreement with Archie was that I should obtain parity of payment, i.e. equal shares, if or when my patient list equalled his. He had a huge flying start, as all Dr. White's patients were automatically placed on his list. I netted then about £450 per annum.

Luck smiled on me again – an elderly lady doctor, Dr. Jane Miller, had been running a small practice in New Road, Ayr, only half a mile from Archie's house. The premises were converted from a shop and Dr. Jane 'lived above the shop'. She could not understand why she was not allowed to charge her patients following the inception of the NHS, so was in dire trouble making ends meet. She was, in any case, fairly well on in years. So, one day, I approached Dr. Miller with a view to buying her house. The NHS as I said, now made purchase of Goodwill illegal.

My wonderful father-in-law again came to the rescue and guaranteed a mortgage, so I purchased 107/109 New Road, Ayr, for £3,000.0s.0d.

We were very strategically placed for the nearby housing schemes and people flocked to the new Surgery – 'The Shop' as it was known. I accepted all comers and, with the aid of our Secretary, Dorothy Bell, my chemist friend's daughter, we were soon piling in the patients. It was a 'free-for-all' then amongst the Ayr General Practitioners building up practices, but there was no competitiveness since the choice of doctor was entirely that of the patient. The approximate income per patient on one's list was in the region of 30 shillings per annum, before tax, and had to be split between Partners.

So, Aileen and I, with Bruce aged about 2 and baby Tricia, moved into our new home where we lived for the next four years, during which time Susan Mary arrived on 19th May 1951 and, eventually, Amanda Gerrard joined the happy family circle on 13th November 1953. About this time, after one of our regular summer holidays of wonderfully happy memories in Connemara and Dublin, it was decided that Tricia should stay behind with her grandparents for a while. Aileen was very hard pressed at the time, as a Dentist as well as a wife and mother – to say nothing of being a General Practitioner's wife. The Digbys and their lovely faithful Nora Fahy, who was their loyal helper from the early Twenties until she died in the Seventies, said at the time to Aileen, "We will keep this baby for ever if you don't take her back quickly!"

Shortly before we moved into 107/109 New Road, Ayr, my Mother, Kathleen, Robert and Campbell left Campbellfield, Irvine, for a beautiful house, Rowantree Cottage, Loans, by Troon. The house was much more suitable for them than Campbellfield, whose upkeep, house and garden, was by now impossible to manage on Granny's meagre pension. This lovely house was a very happy home for Granny Walker until she died peacefully and happily in 1979, aged 91. Granny and Kathleen – Kathleen never married, were constant companions and really good friends. Kathleen totally and unselfishly looked after Granny in the most devoted manner possible.

In the garden ~ Rowantree Cottage
after a Sunday lunch ~ Sixties

The Catholic Faith

*A*fter Granny Walker and Kathleen moved into Rowantree Cottage, Aileen and the children, having been to church at first in St. Margaret's in Ayr and latterly St. Quivox in Prestwick, every Sunday, would make their way to the cottage for lunch. In those days, a lot of my mates would congregate at Troon Golf Club for a regular Sunday morning round. Our children had all been christened in the Catholic faith in St. Margaret's Church, Ayr, by Monsignor McHardie, a grand old man. I gradually felt the odd man out not attending church on Sunday mornings, so I started joining the family there. I felt even more the odd man out as a non-Catholic whilst in the church.

I'm sure Aileen's prayers helped, but I gradually became convinced that I should take instruction in the Catholic faith. I attended sessions with our Parish Priest, Father Breen, and was also tremendously influenced by a Passionist Father from Coodham, near Prestwick, a lovely old mansion house, now sadly a ruin. The Priest was Father Aquinas who took his name from St. Thomas Aquinas.

And so it was, I became a Catholic, which may have raised a few eyebrows, but I was never conscious of any criticism or disapproval, although some parts of Scotland were sectarian. Fortunately, this never raised its ugly head to anything like the extent of the intolerance that still sadly still goes on in Northern Ireland. I am, to this day, increasingly puzzled by the fact that both Protestants and Catholics pray assiduously for Unity amongst Christian Churches, but although we are moving towards this goal due to the strength of Ecumenism, it is still a long way off.

Although I am now a Catholic, I find worship in a Presbyterian or Anglican Church just as meaningful as in a Catholic Church, though I am not supposed to!

Both Catholics and Protestants when taking the Sacrament of Holy Communion are obeying Jesus' order to 'Do This In Memory Of Me'. But centuries ago, the Reformers apparently rejected the concept of 'Transubstantiation', whereby Catholics believe that Christ is actually present in the Bread and Wine. Thus, to this day, Catholics are told that Holy Communion outside of the Catholic Church is flawed.

I really do not perceive that my emotional involvement in Holy Communion as a Catholic is any different from what it was when I was a Protestant. The words 'Do this in memory of me' are identical, but the words apparently do not mean what they say if the Priest is a non-Catholic. What misery and suffering has ensued by this fundamental split in the Christian Churches, surely the exact antithesis of Christ's own teaching when He was so intolerant of the Pharisees strict and repressive interpretation of 'The Law'. I personally get over the problem by believing that The Holy Spirit is in the Bread and Wine and the Holy Spirit is part of the Trinity of The Father, The Son and The Holy Ghost – Three in One and One in Three.

Thus, the Bread and Wine are glorified by the Sacrament. A very good friend, a Catholic Priest, greatly helped my dilemma, even although it appeared to run counter to the strict disciplinary teaching of the Catholic Hierarchy.

More thoughts on Religion

Every star that we see is or has been a Sun, like our own Sun, with a solar system of its own planets.

Jesus Christ was sent to Earth for our salvation as the 'only begotten Son of God'. So, it seems to follow that, because we assume that Beings with life in them, possibly somewhat similar to Beings on our Earth, never have existed or will exist, or, if they did exist, or do exist, God saw, or sees, no necessity to save them from themselves, if our Jesus Christ was his only Son.

Our Parish Priest and friend, Canon Vincent Walker, when listening to my postulations, wisely said, "Percy, I have enough trouble on this planet without worrying about others."

We humans on Earth are probably last in the line of evolution from tiny particles of protoplasm, to the amazing complexity of modern man. Will we evolve further? Do we need to? With the aid of man-made machines, we can move over and under water, fly in the air and in space.

It seems to be that, having reached the stage of self-determination and reasoning, God, seeing the necessity to save his beloved creation from destruction, sent his Son to save them by His example. If we disregard Christ's message, we may suffer the same fate as the dinosaurs, even if the planet Earth itself escapes nemesis.

Talking about Holidays

*I*n the summers and at Christmas time in our early years of marriage, Aileen, the children, when they were very young, and I always went to Ireland for our holidays. The Digbys of Mill House, Dundrum, were incredibly hospitable, and looking back on it, also incredibly tolerant of such an invasion. We took their tolerance for granted, but nevertheless gratefully and of necessity, accepted their immense kindness in relieving us of the problem of finance – they must have known that we had nothing to spare!

Part of the Irish holiday would be in Dublin in the lovely Mill House. Nora, like Granny and Grandpa, was always loving and kind – Nora having been with the family from her own youth until her death.

'Dig' had laid out a most testing 'pitch and putt' course in the garden of Mill House. Although he was not a serious 18-hole golfer, he was a wizard and would regularly be a par buster, beating those who fancied themselves as golfers – such as my brother Robert and our great friend Crawford Gray, both of whom took part in the British Amateur Championship at Portmarnock one year.

The children had an idyllic time playing in the dinghy on the Pond, riding lessons at the Dudgeon's Riding School and, earlier in their lives, being taught to walk by Grandpa Digby. Then we would all go to the West.

JPD owned a series of lakes (lochs, as we would say in Scotland). He was extremely keen on not only fishing, but also on conservation and the promotion of fishing as a major tourist attraction for Ireland, as well as employment for the Irish countrymen in their own land. He felt passionately that the constant flow of Irish people, of both sexes, to Britain was disastrous for the Irish economy and he wrote a most erudite book on the subject: "Emigration – the Answer" – the 'answer' being how to keep the Irish employed in their own land on the land. He would be a happy man now to see Ireland so prosperous financially, even if the prosperity is based largely on the country being a prime mover and shaker in the financial markets of Europe and beyond.

Mill House, Dundrum, Dublin ~ mid Sixties
Aileen and our three daughters, with Grandpa and Granny Digby

So, with Aileen and myself fishing, taking turns to be in J.P.'s boat, rowed by John Dillon or Pat Feeny, we caught many brown trout in Ballynahown Lake and sea trout (called white trout in Ireland) in Upper and Lower Tully Lakes.

* * *

*Grandpa and Granny Digby, Aileen and Bruce
and Barry the Labrador ~ Mill House*

Kids in a dinghy ~ The Pond ~ Mill House

Pat Feeny's (Boatman's) Cottage ~ Ballynahown Lake
Connemara - Demolishment in progress!

Granny Walker with the grandchildren
Rowantree Cottage ~ circa 1957

Nora Fahy with four children on Bentfield Beach ~ 1955

The children were usually with their first cousins, children of Aileen's brother Dillon and his wife June – Jane, Sarah, Simon and Mark (Anna not yet!) – brother Myles and his wife Nancy, and Caroline, (twins Annabel and Anthony not yet!) and often Patricia, sister of Aileen with husband Desmond Mayne and their one and only Bartley. This lot, under the watchful eye of Nora and wee Babs and sometimes other girls, would play endlessly on the hallowed ground and lovely beaches where their parents before them had done likewise when spending their holidays at Granny Laine's lovely home at Inverin nearby.

Home of Granny Laine ~ Aileen's maternal Grandmother
Inverin, County Galway – large extension at back of house not visible

Having been well and truly indoctrinated into Lake fishing in Connemara, we, much later, had wonderful holidays in the Scottish Highland rivers, fishing for salmon. We did little to deplete their numbers!

Other holidays were spent skiing. We made several forays to the rapidly developing ski slopes of the Spey Valley staying sometimes at Aviemore, Boat of Garten, Carr-Bridge or Grantown-on-Spey. Both parents and children learned the basics of skiing there from the legendary Karl Fuchs, and the young very soon outstripped the old in skill.

Aileen fishing on the River Conon ~ 1990

Aileen and I had two wonderful skiing holidays, firstly in Alpbach in Bavaria and secondly, in St. Anton in the Austrian Arlbeg when we were joined by Patricia, Desmond and Bartley Mayne. Years later, we were back in the Arlbeg at a place called Lech, for a lovely holiday with Bruce, Nicky, Digby, Roland and Magnus accompanied by their lovely Filipino lady, Leonie.

I remember one year, Aileen and I had a great holiday touring the Continent in our new car, the aforementioned Ford Popular. We made for Biarritz, down the west coast of France from Le Havre, our landfall, on to Lourdes and then along the Mediterranean Coast. Our home on this trip was a small tent – Tricia was about six months in situ with three to go! Bruce would be parked with Granny Walker and Kathleen in Rowantree Cottage.

Skiing at La Feclaz, French Alps ~ 1995

Later, as well as our Irish trips which were at least once a year, we took our main summer holidays, now with a splendid new Jamet tent, with every possible aid to comfort and haute cuisine, to various parts of Europe – France, Spain, Germany and Austria. It was all great fun, in spite of the time when our Vauxhall Victor's engine blew up on a German autobahn. Our luck held, however, when our AA Gold Star Insurance paid not only for the hire of a Camper Van, but also for a replacement engine for Victor. The AA were marvellous when they realised that we genuinely thought that Victor was fit for the trip and not in a terminal state, which would have been cheating.

Eventually, when the children left school and went to University, they went their own ways with friends for their own holidays.

One very special and memorable trip took place in 1966, when we were exceedingly lucky to join an Ampleforth College pilgrimage to Russia, together with boys, Bruce included, and Monks from Ampleforth. We took the train from Victoria, the ferry across the Channel from Folkestone to Boulogne, then a train all the way to Berlin where we had a quick look around East Berlin.

This was a frightening experience. We took half a dozen boys across on the over-ground railway through the Checkpoint into the East. Bruce was not with us, as his passport was in his suitcase in the Left Luggage Office. On arrival in Berlin Eastern Zone, we had to surrender our passports and purchase some East German money, which was not convertible back into West German Marks. We had a look around – the area was desolate, still bare with broken down, old buildings, a huge contrast to West Berlin in every way.

When we got back to the Friedrichstrasse Railway Station in the East for a train for the West, only a mile or so away, we were met by huge crowds trying to get on the train. Only those with passes or passports had any hope of getting into the Western zone. The passport numbers were being read out in German. Fortunately, I had learnt enough German at school to recognise our name and passport numbers, so we managed to get on the last train of the day on this suburban line.

The Monks were in a dreadful panic, understandably, waiting for our return with at least half a dozen boys, as we had to catch the Moscow train from Berlin Ost shortly after our safe return. We journeyed from Berlin to Moscow via Warsaw. At the Polish Russian frontier, Brest Litovsk, our train had to have its wheels adjusted to the Russian wider gauge, which entailed hoisting up the carriages by crane and exchanging the smaller gauge bogies for the larger ones. We had comfortable four-berth sleeping cars that made for a very smooth journey to Moscow.

It was Easter time. The object of the trip was to concelebrate Mass with the Russian Orthodox Church. This was, I believe, the very first concelebrated Mass between Rome and Russian Orthodoxy since the ancient churches had split centuries before. The ceremony took place in a Hotel bedroom, with our Ampleforth Priests and the son of the Russian Orthodox Metropolitan in London, Voloda, together with three Russian Orthodox Hierarchy.

Later, it was a very moving experience to see the religious fervour of the Russians. The believers were in the minority in this Communist country that officially banned all Christian worship. The elderly Russians were astonished and emotional at seeing young people in a Church. The Easter Sunday service was in the Pro Cathedral in Moscow. The wonderful deep bass voices of the huge bearded Orthodox priests and the evocative music and song are luckily recorded on an LP record, as I had a tape recorder concealed under my raincoat.

Our entry into the Cathedral was very strongly resisted by some young protesters, who were eventually and forcibly removed by the Police. The service took nearly three hours and there are no seats in Russian churches!

We saw lots of wonderful sights in Moscow including a performance of *Swan Lake* in a huge hall within the Kremlin. It was on this occasion that, when we returned to our bus after the performance, we discovered that Aileen was missing! After collecting our coats from the cloakroom – it was compulsory to remove your coat before entering the Theatre – the walkway propelled us to either one door exit or another. By the time Aileen had collected her coat, the points had changed on the walkway and she found herself alone in Red Square, directly on the opposite side of the huge Kremlin compound, whilst the others were all in the bus at the Spanish Riding School. A kindly Russian policeman spotted Aileen's distress and there followed an exchange of words, entirely unintelligible. It so happened that as Moscow Dynamos had beaten Glasgow Rangers recently, this became a password to international relations between the two. But that was not getting Aileen back to the bus, so she started galloping like a Lipizaner horse and whinnying and beating her bottom, and then the penny dropped. She was escorted to the bus at the Spanish Riding School to the huge relief of all, including Valentina, who would have been sent to the salt mines as well as losing her Intourist job if she had lost one of her charges.

We visited many wonderful ancient buildings, especially churches, whose interiors had been stripped of any sign of religious usage. Before leaving Moscow we went on a long coach journey to Zagorsk, which was an ancient seminary and monastery – one of the few where the Orthodox Priests were permitted to practise their vocation.

Our next stop was Leningrad, now again St. Petersburg, by overnight train. There we saw wonderful buildings, including the Hermitage Palace, a museum containing a lot of the world's greatest artistic treasures and paintings. We also saw the cruiser *Aurora* whose guns had proclaimed the Bolshevik Revolution in, I think, 1917.

A most moving sight was the War Memorial to the millions of Russians who lost their lives when the Nazis only just failed to capture the city, having reached a few miles from the city walls.

We then flew by Aeroflot to Riga in Latvia, where we embarked on a Russian ship, the *Nadeska Krupskaya*; the name of Lenin's wife. We had a most adventurous trip home from Riga to Tilbury. First, we became well and truly stuck in the Baltic ice, until an icebreaker from Riga eventually made a passage for our escape.

Further excitement on board the *Nadeska Krupskaya* was caused by an explosive mixture of schools from Britain, being of different religious denominations, but especially very varied social status. (Unpleasant words: 'Social Status'.) The higher the status, the more comfortable the living quarters – not a good idea! I only just managed to quell a riot by inviting some very angry young rebels in the bowels of the ship to join us in the First Class bar. They had been freely drinking very cheap brandy in the Second or Third Class bar.

Another mild problem was boy meets girl at sea! However, we arrived at Tilbury on time despite the ice, which saved the Captain's face and his job. It was a great trip.

Illness

I contracted a bug, eventually diagnosed after a long time as Giardia Lamblia. This nearly killed me and defied the best medical brains as to the exact diagnosis. However, after a few weeks, I happened to see an article in the British Medical Journal written by a wartime British Medical Officer who successfully treated his patients in Archangel, I think it was, with Vitamin B12 and folic acid, which saved their lives. I tried this and it saved me, too. I regained my weight from 9st. or thereabouts, to its usual 13½st., and I have never looked back. I was off work for four weeks due to this illness, but had I not been a self-employed GP, it could have been for very much longer.

My absence of four weeks following the Russian Bug was almost the only time I was off work in my entire medical career, both as a student, in the Navy, in hospitals and in General Practice. Sometimes, fortunately not often, I had ordinary minor illnesses, common colds, etc., but how could you stay off work when the only people who could step into the breach were your Partners, who were already up to their necks in work. I was often in a worse state than my patients, who, having decided not to work because they did not feel up to it, required a Certificate of Incapacity from me! Very frustrating!

Referring to our, fortunately, very rare illnesses and absence from work, I vividly recall Aileen being in absolute agony with back pain. This would have be sometime in the sixties. We asked for the opinion of an Orthopaedic Surgeon who thought that it must be a slipped disc and prescribed rest and sedation. This back pain followed a severe upper respiratory infection, which had given rise to acute sinus pain. At the time, Aileen was working in various hospitals, in addition to her own practice as a Dentist. One was the Biggart Hospital in Prestwick, where she looked after the dental care of very under-privileged children from poor homes in Glasgow. The Biggart Hospital was named after a Glasgow philanthropist, Mr. Biggart. Shortly after the acute back pain and the sinus infection, it became more and more obvious that there was more to Aileen's problem. By chance, when Aileen was walking down a corridor in Ayr Hospital, she was spotted by Dr. Robert Hill, Consultant Physician, and Mr Gordon Watt, the Orthopaedic Surgeon. They both saw Aileen staggering and realised that she was in far more trouble than hitherto diagnosed. Very soon she became totally paralysed in both legs, which required her to lie on her back for weeks on end in the hospital. You can imagine how worried we all were. A good friend of mine, Dr. Robert Sommerville, who was the son of one of my skin chiefs of student days, immediately pinpointed the problem from samples that I took up to him in Belvedere Hospital, Glasgow. It was a virus infection similar to what was sweeping through the poorer areas of Glasgow, especially amongst children. Aileen's weakened state with the sinus infection had greatly lowered her resistance to this prevalent Coxackie A7 virus. It had caused the agonising back pain and severely affected the motor nerve supply to her legs, hence a paralysis very similar to that of poliomyelitis. To my intense delight, Robbie Sommerville was 100% optimistic. He said, "It's a Coxackie A7 infection," even though he had no concrete proof. Most of the specimens had proved negative to all the available tests at the time. He told me that Aileen would get completely better, which she did, although it took a long time and one leg remained a lot weaker for ages.

Apart from Aileen's wartime typhoid and later, this Coxackie poliomyelitis and my Giardia Lamblia, the 'Russian bug', we have been and still are, amazingly healthy specimens. It seems that on the rare occasion that a doctor or his family gets ill, they make a meal of it!

Sailing

Over the years, we have had great fun sailing and enjoyed some great sailing holidays. We were a regular crew with good friends who lived in Troon, John and Josie Chapman. They kept a boat, *Liz*, a South Coast One Design cutter at Fairlie, where we had a lot of cruises and races with the Clyde Cruising Club.

We later took up dinghy sailing and started with an Enterprise, by the name of *Walkover*. At first, we were always capsizing in this very fast and tender boat, but we eventually improved, especially when Aileen took my place at the helm! We were founder members of Prestwick Sailing Club just along the promenade from *Bentfield*, about half a mile away. On Saturdays and Sundays, we had a lot of fun racing round the buoys at the Club against Enterprises and GP14s. We also had a very small 100 Class, I think it was, dinghy called *Centime*, which we kept at Ayr Bay Sailing Club, but we sold her when we joined the Prestwick Sailing Club.

After the Enterprise, which sadly more or less disintegrated, we bought a *Mirror* that we still have, and occasionally sail. We keep her in good shape for the family when they are at *Bentfield* with us.

When the Chapmans left Troon, they bought another yacht, this time an all steel hulled boat quite a bit longer than *Liz* called *Genever*, named after Dutch Gin – appropriate! We had wonderful trips in *Genever*, both across the channel from their homeport, Christchurch, and to France and the Channel Isles. The Whitsunday race from Poole to Cherbourg was quite memorable, but most of my memories are unrepeatable in this journal!

WALKOVER on Prestwick Beach ~ early Eighties
Note: Granny Digby below

Mirror dinghy – Bentfield ~ mid Nineties
Jessica, Emma, Oliver, Ian, Aileen, Tricia

Whitsunday Race on Chapman's GENEVER ~ 1965
Cherbourg Harbour

To conclude my sailing memories, I must not forget our Caribbean Cruise with John and Tricia Kennedy in their 45ft. yacht, *Cinderella*. I think this was in 1987. They had just crossed the Atlantic with several friends, a month or so before we joined them in Nelson's Harbour, Antigua. We had a marvellous time visiting the Islands of Barbuda, Nevis and St. Kitts in glorious weather. On the way home we dropped in to see great friends Dermot and Toiny Nee who were Irish relations of Aileen, their home being in Naples, Florida, where we received their usual incredible hospitality.

CANTAMAR at anchorage in 'The Garvellachs'
Islands off the West Coast of Scotland ~ mid Nineties

(A lovely cruise in John and Tricia Kennedy's boat)

Early Days of the NHS

*H*aving digressed about holidays and sailing, I must go back to the Fifties. Work in our practice became busier and busier. When one of us was on holiday, the workload of the other was overwhelming. To mitigate the pressure of work greatly, however, I was tremendously inspired by a book written at that time by a Dr. Taylor, whom I think later became Lord Taylor of Gryffe. The book was called 'Good General Practice'. By following its precepts to the letter, we initiated a well-organised system of record keeping. Prior to that, our medical record envelopes, which were provided by the Executive Council of the NHS, were empty and stuffed away and forgotten. So, being well organised was a tremendous help to getting through the work without constantly chasing one's tail while lurching from one crisis to another.

In those early days of the NHS, initiated on 4 July 1948, the contrast in my ability to give patients what they required and deserved, was in total contrast to my experiences pre-NHS, even taking into account my own enhanced abilities. There was virtually no limit to what a doctor could prescribe free of charge and with no consultation fees. The peripheral hospitals were no longer staffed by GP Consultants. They, in their day, had done a marvellous job, with a great spread of skills, but Medicine was advancing so rapidly that the newly created posts had to be filled by full time and highly qualified specialists.

The advent of the Sulfa drugs and, later, antibiotics, was an enormous leap from time-honoured treatments of the past into the era of wonder drugs. There was a tendency, irresistibly, to prescribe antibiotics for everything from a mild common cold to severe feverish illnesses, without an accurate diagnosis. No doubt whatever, that although unscientific, we either knowingly, or usually unknowingly, saved our patients from what had formerly been killer diseases and much morbidity as well.

There was, and still is, a plus and a minus regarding the new so easy access to a doctor. We were able to spot illness at a very much earlier stage and with a very much greater chance of success. With such a flood of patient contacts, it could sometimes be difficult to differentiate between trivial complaints that would be better served without any treatment, and complaints, which first appeared trivial, but very soon were not. So 'better safe than sorry' influenced our prescribing habits greatly. I always remembered my 'guru' in my early days of General Practice, Dr. Alex Gibson of Irvine, saying, "Never argue with a patient or criticise them – they are the ones who drop dead." Good advice! Instead of being critical or touchy about being called out in anti-social hours, I had a fail-safe method. Attend the call as soon as possible, be pleasant and non-committal and say, "I will look in tomorrow morning to see how you are." I used to make my second visit as early as I could, often being out in the wee small hours anyway. That cured them!

We had a very large number of pregnant mums, being the pre-pill era. We gave meticulous ante-natal care and delivered the babies in a purpose built cottage-type maternity hospital, Thorneyflat in Ayr. When I say I delivered the babies, I attended the confinements as soon as possible, but was more than happy to let the midwives do the actual work. They were much better at it than any doctor. Of course, their terms of service limited them to normal cases. In complicated cases, the doctor had to step in with or without help from the experts in the Central Hospital in Irvine.

I found that, by and large, if the doctors treated patients with respect and consideration, the patients treated the doctors similarly.

Archie and I were extremely lucky to find a new recruit to our practice, Ernest Armitage, whose father had been a revered Cumnock GP. I had known Ernest in my Ballochmyle days when he, newly qualified, was there with me whilst I was doing my post-war postgraduate posts. In the meantime, Ernest had been doing his National Service in British Somaliland, now Somalia and had recently obtained his Membership of The Royal College of Physicians. His wife Mary, née Auld, was also a qualified doctor.

This was the start of a very happy threesome in the Practice. Ernest's higher degree gave Archie and myself some incentive to be as knowledgeable as Ernest was. The sharing of the workload was a great boon and by this time, we all agreed that equal work must be rewarded by equal pay – a concept that was creeping in everywhere since the inception of the NHS.

Our patient lists still kept growing healthily and to augment our income, we took on the medical care of Butlin's Holiday Camp, near Ayr, the very same place where Aileen had had her first Naval experience when it was *HMS Scotia*. Dr. Mary Armitage did a daily surgery at Butlin's, which at the peak of the season, had up to 3,000 holidaymakers. We were paid ten shillings by the NHS per patient contact, regardless of the severity or otherwise of the illness. This was half the payment for a Temporary Resident treated elsewhere other than the Camp. I fought unsuccessfully for this anomaly to be rectified.

After a few years of Butlin's, during which time a bonus was free admission with our children to the Camp and its facilities, we did some arithmetic and concluded that financially, we were only running to stand still. So we withdrew from Butlin's. No other practice took it on. The numbers of campers attending the sick bay dropped dramatically in the absence of a doctor, and I am sure that, if anything, the general health of the camp improved as they had better things to do than to go sick! I think there may be a moral here – nationally.

By now, to our great joy, Susan Mary had arrived. When we purchased 109 New Road, Ayr, from Dr. Jane Miller. She asked us if we would keep on her old housekeeper who lived nearby (at 48 Viewfield Road). We agreed with pleasure, because we had already discovered that this wee lady, Mrs. Barbara Halliday, adored children. She had married a Mr. Halliday, who was much older than herself and they never had any children of their own. She was a loving, faithful Nanny to all four children from that day, until she took ill and died many years later. 'Wee Babs' used to take Bruce, Tricia and Susan, together with Topper the fox terrier, for a walk every day, (the youngest baby, Amanda, being in the pram. She was, of course, a wonderful help to Aileen who, having built the Dental Surgery at the back of 107/109, was very busy as a Doctor's wife, a Dentist and a mother. It was wonderful for our children to have such a lady as Wee Babs to be their friend and carer in these early days and she looked after the parents as well!

Regarding Aileen's Dental work, she had, in the early days of our marriage, worked with the Ayr County Council School Dental Service. This involved travelling by bus to various clinics in Ayrshire. Morning sickness (Bruce) sometimes made this journey stressful!

In 1950, we constructed a purpose-built Dental Surgery on to the back of the Medical Surgery, where Aileen ran her own practice until her retiral.

In addition, she did weekly Dentist Sessions at two local hospitals – Heathfield and The Biggart.

Nanny, Mrs Barbara Halliday ~ Wee Babs
with her charges and Aileen & Topper
Bruce about to go to Carlekemp School ~ September 1957
(Note bare, bleak Bentfield)

Percy and his Water Babes

Bentfield

*O*ne day, Aileen spotted an advertisement in the *Ayrshire Post*: For Sale – Property known as *Bentfield*, Maryborough Road, Prestwick. 107/109 was bursting at the seams, with three children, and being a very busy medical and dental surgery. Amanda arrived to our great pleasure on 13 November 1953. I was golfing one afternoon; it must have been a Thursday, when a message came from Aileen via a caddy, who ran out on to the course calling, "*Bentfield* is for sale."

One wet Saturday about a year previously, I wanted to hear the Aintree Grand National on the radio. There was then a lot of interference due to cable problems on our mains radio in the house, so I got into the car. Aileen was minding the phone and the children. I went along a deserted Newton-on-Ayr promenade where I spotted a bleak, gaunt house on a headland bounded by St. Nicholas Golf course and the sea. Neither of us, strangely, had ever noticed this house before. But later though, as soon as we could, we explored the area in which the house stood amidst sand dunes within its own 4 acres. Too good to be true! The house looked derelict and appeared to be uninhabited. In fact, it was occupied by personnel from the United States Air Base at Prestwick, who had battened themselves down against the prevailing gales off the sea. We made enquiries at the Lodge and were told who the owner was.

When the advertisement appeared in the local paper, I went straight to the owner to assess our chances. The owner was a Mr. Hector McArthur, a local builder and joiner. He owned both *Bentfield House* with its Lodges and the adjacent *Bellrock House*, immediately north of *Bentfield*. Mr. McArthur was very non-

153

committal and said, "Come back in a few months when I know what I intend to do." We could hardly wait – every day, we dreamt about our dream house. Aileen threw a Miraculous Medal over the wall, which I am sure helped. Eventually, we could stand it no longer. I went to see Hector who said he had not done anything more about it – "Make me an offer". With the advice of our Solicitor, Jim Penny of McMillan and Howie, an old Ayr firm of Lawyers, I made him an offer. The sum is a secret, but a lot less than its present day value. The deal was 'signed' and *Bentfield* was ours in the summer of 1953.

Bentfield is a very well built house. Thick walls of sandstone, beautiful plaster cornices in the main rooms and superb wood-work. It had been very neglected, but the neglect was superficial. We spent many long hours scraping off thick, old wallpaper and paint, both inside and out. Beautiful pine had been smothered in paint inside whilst the outside paint was badly peeling and cracked.

Bare, bleak, Bentfield
when we bought it in 1953

Again, my wonderful father-in-law came to the rescue. He and his wife Jean had come across the Irish Sea to see *Bentfield* for themselves. They were both ecstatic, even if the house and garden were a mess. The situation was then and is still unique. We have an uninterrupted view of the Firth of Clyde, taking in the whole of Arran and stretching from the Heads of Ayr to the South of Bute. So, J.P. Digby again gave me all the financial backing required, the interest on which I assiduously paid back in instalments as agreed. Archie was as keen as I was to make 107/109 the surgery for the Partnership, so I sold him a half share in the property. Ernest eventually became a partner, when we shared one third each of the property.

There was a huge amount to be done in *Bentfield* which we did by honing our DIY skills and greatly helped by wonderful skilled tradesmen especially Alex Cowan, father and son, joiners. Alex Junior was only allowed a motorised vehicle after 'Senior' retired!

Prior to that, they pushed a handcart from Ayr with all their tools and equipment on board. It is amazing to look back at our cashbooks to see the cost of tradesmen's bills in the early Fifties compared with today, even after adjusting for new money and inflation.

We set about cutting the grass, a lot of it. This was the only thing growing in the whole four acres, marram grass or Bents – hence the name of the house.

J.P. Digby gave us a present of an Atcoscythe Motor Mower; this was before the invention of the Flymos. We realised that, in this extremely exposed place to both wind and salt spray, that we could never have a garden until we established a shelter belt. So, we embarked on an ambitious, most people would say impossible, task of aforestation. In our first year, I planted 1,000 young conifer seedlings, which were lodge poles and Contorta Pines. The death rate was about 90% per annum, but I persevered and each year had more and more survivors. I learnt that to survive, each tree had to have a deep hole in the sand, all the sand removed and replaced by good loam compost, and each tree had to have adequate shelter with Netlon protective netting.

Bentfield Garden – South West aspect ~ 1954

Aileen had spotted lorries coming and going from the new outpatient Hospital Clinic at Heathfield nearby. The lorries were carting away wonderful topsoil, as the building site had been allotments previously. She persuaded the contractor to dump this 'windfall' of soil where we wanted it, which they were delighted to do, thus saving themselves money and at no cost to ourselves. The 'garden' before this had been on pure sand.

Year after year, we watched our wee trees growing slowly but surely, sometimes not. But we won in the end, and now have impenetrable woodland except for our view of the sea from the house, which we kept free of trees. Wild roses, the dog rose, Rosa

Canina, also became an impenetrable windbreak, which we planted from little sticks, but now have to be controlled and cut back. Our garden gradually evolved inside the windbreaks and in the hollows surrounding the house. Although wind and salt are still a big problem, we have a great variety of shrubs and plants that thrive, helped by our relatively frost-free situation due to the proximity of the Gulf Stream.

Azaleas *Bentfiel* *d in* *and* *Pl--- h---*

The Practice

*H*aving moved, lock, stock and barrel from the Surgery, we were now able to redesign its interior, retaining the Dental Surgery for Aileen, which we had already added to the building. We also kept the upstairs living quarters as a caretaker flat where Mr. and Mrs. Kenneth Robson dwelt and were as helpful and kindly people as one would wish for.

In due course, our next-door neighbours in 111 New Road, Mrs. Wright and family, decided to emigrate to Australia. They were delighted to sell the other part of the attached building, so we did more redesigning of the interior, joining both houses into one. At this time, our purchase of the new building was financed by taking in a partner, a single-handed General Practitioner, already a very good friend, Dr. Thomas Rutherford. So Tommy brought all his patients from across the road to join our list and became a quarter shareholder in the practice premises.

During the period from acquiring 107/109 New Road, until the mid-Sixties, we were rather ahead of our time by initiating attachments of Queen's District Nurses, Midwives and Health Visitors to the Practice. This was an uphill struggle, as the Medical Officer of Health for the Royal Burgh of Ayr; Dr. Robert Leask, was very reluctant to let his nurses work for us instead of the Burgh Clinics, which are now non-existent. We were also ahead of our time with the Appointments System. Previously, it was first come, first served, when the clever ones piled in at the end of surgery hours, just before the door was shut! We also made it our duty to carry the patients records with us on house calls whenever possible, or, at least, to write up case notes as soon as possible thereafter. This may seem elementary, but it was certainly necessary and is now mandatory in an age when treatment and diagnosis are so much more sophisticated.

We also had a gigantic task in gradually transferring all our patient records from the old small envelopes to A4 size folders. It became totally impossible to squeeze a fraction of the records into such a small space in the old envelopes. As a result, we had to make room for the much bigger records. Computerised records were well after my time.

We spent a lot of time and money adapting the building to the ever-expanding needs of a modern practice. Archie had sadly and suddenly, lost his charming wife, the Belgian, Myriam, and after the Wright's departure, Archie lived in the upstairs room of 111. Nessie McCaffer, who had been Aileen's Dental Assistant, and her husband, Hugh, were in the old quarters upstairs above 109, as both Robsons had died.

Soon after the upstairs rooms were utilised for surgery premises, we rented a room one or two days a week to our Gynaecologist colleagues from Irvine, where they saw their private patients.

Archie and Tommy retired in 1979 and 1980 respectively. I instituted a scheme, wisely I am sure, whereby the retiring doctors gave up all night and weekend work during their final years in the Practice. We made up for our lost services by taking in a young partner, paid for partly by Government assistance and partly from money that the old partner had given up as a result of a lighter workload. This arrangement worked very well. We were very lucky to obtain splendid new partners who also, to some extent, absorbed our best traditions and superseded our worst ones.

The three young doctors, by 2002, had become the senior members of a six-doctor partnership, which flourishes as the Tam's Brig Surgery. The building has been totally refurbished and enlarged since I left!

I was pleasantly surprised and honoured to be appointed Deputy Lieutenant for Ayr and Arran just before my retirement in 1981.

A super state-of-the art hospital has been built on the outskirts of Ayr. This opened in 1991 to replace the old Ayr County Hospital, which was chiefly surgical, whilst the old Heathfield Hospital, which was mainly medical and the old Seafield Hospital which was for children. The new hospital, The Ayr Hospital, is a few miles from the centre of Ayr, adjacent to the old Glengall Lunatic Asylum now renamed Ailsa Hospital. Formerly, the new hospital would have been far too remote, but nowadays, with car ownership so widespread, even its enormous car park is always full! During my medical career, I have seen the transition in the Glengall Lunatic Asylum, from the straitjacket if you were 'off your head' to a mental illness no longer being stigmatised. There have been enormous strides in the treatment and care of the psychiatrically disturbed patient and in the welfare of mentally retarded patients.

Ancillary Staff

I cannot overestimate the importance of good Reception and Clerical Staff in a General Practice. We could not have been luckier.

So, between the ages of 60 and 65 years, I was able to shed the most arduous part of general practice, i.e. out of hours work. I am sure it prolonged my active life, as it is now 20 years or more since I retired. On retirement, I felt far too young and active to be on the shelf.

I had had a toehold in the DHSS – Department of Health and Social Security – whilst still working as a GP and now I was again lucky to obtain almost a full-time job doing Industrial Injury Medical Boards, together with a travelling job of going to peoples' homes the length and breadth of Ayrshire and Arran, to assess claimants for the Attendance Allowance and Mobility Allowance. I found this work extremely interesting, as well as being better paid for less work! It also allowed me to augment my NHS Pension. I concluded that increasing a person's income was very much more efficacious than prescribing pills and far less costly. I really enjoyed seeing such a large variety of people, especially the former Ayrshire miners and their families, who were the salt of the earth. I suppose that their life of hardship contributed to this. I was obliged to give up this job at the age of 72.

My work as a GP in the National Health Service gave me great job satisfaction. However, the NHS remains an ever-open mouth, ready and able to swallow an ever-increasing amount of money.

The National Health Service

$\mathcal{T}$he National Health Service was a great social experiment. The politicians of the day, of all parties, realised at various times following the Industrial Revolution that things must change dramatically as regards the welfare and well-being of the workers. Whereas previously, landowners and the wealthy in general, felt responsible for their tenants and workers' welfare, with the arrival of the industrial revolution with its 'dark satanic mills'; coal mines and foundries, the living conditions of the masses, who toiled impossibly long hours, even the young children, were absolutely scandalous. True, some employers were enlightened, but they were in the minority. In spite of medical insurance schemes, into which both workers and employers paid a small sum weekly to cover sickness or injury, the bulk of the nation was not covered for illnesses or emergencies. Many, or most doctors, pre-National Health days, had a sliding scale of fees – they waived a fee in cases of extreme poverty and charged pro rata according to a patient's financial and social status. But, even allowing for the doctor's generosity, the poor, who were the majority, could not, and often did not, afford medical attention until illness was really serious and far advanced. Likewise, injuries usually meant termination of employment, although the Workers' Compensation Act did help a bit. So, when Bevan and Beveridge produced their plan in 1948, the expectation was that free treatment, free access to doctors and hospitals, free dental treatment and free appliances etc., would produce a healthy Britain, and that many illnesses would be conquered or eliminated.

Simultaneously, a National Insurance Scheme was inaugurated in 1948, and every person in employment paid a weekly contribution, as would his or her employer. Thus, sickness or injury episodes were rewarded by sickness or injury benefits. Needless to say, the requirement for Certification of Illness required a doctor's examination and a Certificate. This was by no means an exact appraisal of the claimant's health or fitness for work, and not only was it a colossal waste of doctor's time, often for trivial uncertifiable reasons, but it also encouraged absenteeism and resulting over-employment. This alone was a major cause of Britain's inability to compete with other industrial nations. It often paid a worker better to be off work than at work. In spite of the downside, the Scheme was truly of enormous benefit to the whole population. Strangely, those who can now afford private treatment prefer the old system!

Many diseases and conditions, especially infectious diseases, due to bacillary infection, such as Scarlet Fever, Nephritis, Septicaemia, Peritonitis, Mastoiditis, were, by and large, eliminated due to the new wonder drugs like the Sulfas and Penicillin. As I have mentioned before, there was a temptation, impossible then to resist, to prescribe wonder drugs for every febrile illness. We did not realise that we were storing up very serious trouble for the future by this practice. A large proportion of the febrile illnesses, which we treated with antibiotics, still a common practice, were of virus causation. The viruses were, and are, completely immune to antibiotics. 'The continuous use, over the years, of antibiotics has rendered many of them tired or even useless against diseases for which they were once efficacious.' This is a major problem today – we cannot forever find new antibiotics.

Apparently, the original idea of the founders of the National Health Service was that, by reducing the incidence and mortality of sickness episodes, the cost of the Service would reduce. The exact opposite has, of course, happened!

In spite of superhuman efforts of those who work in the NHS, invariably underpaid, the Service costs escalate year in, year out and will do so forever.

The original concept of the National Health Service was free consultations, free prescribing of any medication or appliance. This was admirable, but impossible without adequate funding, so waiting lists become longer and longer and, in consequence, private insurance is often the only way to obtain timely and necessary treatment, if one can afford it. NHS hospitals are now forced to utilise private facilities or send patients to the Continent – what a disgrace! More and more people are moving to private insurance, which, as I have said before, is good for those who can afford it, and it is also good for Private Practitioners.

I often wonder why it is not possible for our politicians to set up a totally new system for providing the ever-increasing finance to run the NHS properly. In a word, why not 'Nationalise' the existing private insurance schemes, making patients' contributions commensurate with both their needs and expectations. This would provide adequate finance to make state-of-the-art hospitals available to rich and poor alike. Maybe I am naïve, but I think politicians are already exploring these ideas through absolute necessity. There is a precedent for the nationalisation of Private Medical Insurance. In July 1948, what had been private insurance through so-called 'Friendly Societies', became overnight, an integral part of new National Insurance and National Health contributions.

As I think I said before, one of the effects of the National Health Service has been to some extent the erosion of old fashioned self-reliance. If our Nation could regain its former self-reliance, this would drastically cut down a lot of waste of doctors' time and resources. I do not know what the answer is, but I do know that my successors are rapidly becoming an endangered species.

I escaped the era of paper mountains, created by the present obsession of Governments with accountability. Accountability is eroding the GP's job satisfaction and independence.

Royal College of General Practitioners

I must mention the Royal College of General Practitioners. This organisation was set up in the fifties by a group of enthusiasts, many of them academics with higher degrees. They could see a great future for General Practice if a College could be set up, both to train GP's and appraise their performance, as well as setting up very high standards of both actual practice and practice organisation, including research projects. I was imbued with all these innovations. Some GPs, however, belonging to a highly individualistic profession, could not abide what they perceived to be 'elitism' and self-satisfaction, and especially Fellows wearing fancy gowns! This perception was understandable, but entirely false. The College has done and is still doing a vast amount of good for General Practice, largely due to the dedicated Doctors who find time to work both for the College and their Practices.

166

Prestwick Golf Club

I referred previously to Thursday being my half-day from the Practice. Sometimes on a Thursday, Aileen and I would escape to the countryside often travelling miles to favourite spots in the Highlands, happy in the knowledge that the children were safe with Nanny. Other Thursdays and Aileen was very sporting about this, I would play golf at Prestwick. The tradition of friends at Prestwick Golf Club on a Thursday had been in operation for years. Also, Thursday was a day 'when a gentleman could give up his hunting or shooting or fishing pursuits'. I joined this unique Club in 1938, my father already being a member.

Prestwick was, and is, and I am sure always will be, a haven of happiness and good fellowship, playing golf on one of the most prestigious golf courses in the world, steeped in golfing history, including being where the very first Open Championship was played in 1860. Even during my leaves from the Navy, I always homed in to Prestwick Golf Club, often with fellow Officers, Surgeon Lieutenant Peter McCrae (later lost in an Arctic convoy in *HMS Mahratta*) and Surgeon Lieutenant Jos Reynolds. During the war, the other Club that I joined in 1936, Troon, now Royal Troon, was taken over as Combined Operations Headquarters. But in those grim days, my father and his friends still met for fun and golf at the Portland Club, a Club within a Club for Troon townsfolk.

After the war, Prestwick was short of members. Pre-war members were, to a large extent, 'landed gentry' and retired high-ranking officers, now an almost extinct species. Their descendents have to farm their lands themselves. As I said, I was a pre-war member, but many of my friends were lucky enough to be admitted to Prestwick after the war, and moved from Troon because the latter Club was always busy and tended to have games fixed ahead from week to week. One of the very important reasons for the wonderful atmosphere at Prestwick is the tradition of games of golf being arranged spontaneously, and no one is ever left without a game. By this means, the young and the old were mixed up on the links and in the Club, and the young absorbed the traditions of the Club. The 'long table' in the lunchroom was, and is, a great catalyst for all members of all ages to enjoy each other's company. In spite of the changing world, Prestwick Golf Club remains an oasis of sheer pleasure and good fellowship.

Prestwick Golf Club
Pen and ink drawing by my good friend, Donald MacLellan –
showing the Clubhouse after the redevelopment in time for the
Sesquicentennial Celebrations

Even the question of Ladies in Prestwick Golf Club has been successfully resolved, not by lady membership, but by entertaining the ladies in 'non-men-only' parts of the Club, and as our guests on the links.

Prestwick Golf club ~ 2000 (after extension)
Some Walkers: Percy, James, Hugh and Ian

Royal Troon Golf Club ~ which I joined in 1936

Prestwick has matches with Royal Troon, Prestwick St. Nicholas, (a Club which was instituted the same year as Prestwick, 1851) and Prestwick St. Cuthbert. In these games it tends to be the best players in the Clubs who participate.

We also have either annual or bi-annual matches, alternating between home and away, with the Royal and Ancient Golf Club of St. Andrews, The Honourable Company of Edinburgh Golfers (Muirfield), Portmarnock Golf Club in Dublin, and Royal County Down in Northern Ireland. In the latter two matches especially, I have been involved on many occasions when staying power was the reason for my inclusion in the team, rather than golfing skill!

Prestwick Golf Club has been extremely lucky in its Golf Professionals, going back to the beginning in Tom Morris's day, then Charlie Hunter followed by Bob McInnes, and for the last 40 or so years, our great Frank Rennie, who is an institution. We have also been extremely lucky to have had two generations of the Bennett family looking after the inner man, which I am certain is the answer to the wonderful atmosphere at Prestwick. I had the great honour to serve as Captain of Prestwick in the years 1976-77.

I have been extremely fortunate to be elected to the Senior Golfers' Society; a great fraternity of elderly golfers. The earliest one can be elected is after one's 55th birthday and I joined in 1975. This is a really wonderful organisation and by definition, all Seniors are friends of all Seniors. My middle brother, Robert, who has won many competitions in his time, playing golf from scratch, is a Past Captain and President of the Seniors. Sadly, the youngest brother, Campbell, failed to succeed in the Ballot for membership of the Seniors – proof of the Ballots total fairness.

The Cairn, Prestwick Golf Club

*Marking the spot of the first tee in the first Open championship ~ 1860
(note the old clubs)
I was Captain of Prestwick in 1977, when the Cairn was unveiled by
Henry Cotton*

171

Percy in the Smoke Room, Prestwick Golf Club
"Yes – I could manage another pint!"

Race Doctor

$\mathcal{A}$nother flashback to the Fifties! One day, I was approached by Mr. Robert Cormack who had been an Ayr GP and a General Surgeon in the County Hospital in pre-NHS days. He had an appointment as Medical Officer to The Western Meeting Club, situated at Ayr Racecourse, which was Scotland's premier track and still is. Previously, at nearby Bogside, under the Clerk of the Course, was Alex McHarg, who looked after both Bogside and Ayr. Bogside was the National Hunt course; Ayr was then entirely flat, until Bogside closed in the Sixties. One day, Bob Cormack asked me to join him as Assistant Medical Officer at Ayr. I jumped at the chance, and after Cormack's retirement, I remained Senior M.O. for over 30 years, being presented with a lovely carriage clock when I reached 70 in 1986, the age when Racing Officials retire.

In my early days as Race Doctor, there was no such thing as an Injured Jockeys Fund. It was often left to the pressure put on the doctor by the jockey that was the deciding factor as to his fitness to ride, unless the injury was obviously too serious. I remember a jockey defying my advice not to ride, but, with the connivance of the trainer and unknown to the Stewards, he ran with two broken collarbones and won his race! The determination of a somewhat battered jockey to ride in a race was a very good indicator of his likelihood to win and therefore worth a modest bet!

The Racing Game is mysterious and complex, and sometimes was, though not now I think, dodgy without the utmost scrutiny by the Stewards and Officials.

OUT ON TO THE COURSE AT AYR

174

The MO's job was to be in the Stewards' Box during all races and keep his mouth shut until ordered to open it, but, with mutual respect and understanding, enormously aided by the Joint Clerks of the Course, Bill McHarg and Kit Patterson, we absorbed a lot of the nuances of the job.

The National Hunt jockeys are an extraordinary band of chaps. They love their sport and have to take amazing risks by the very nature of their sport. Over the years in which I was involved, 'safety' became much more of a factor, due largely to compensation and litigation. Many innovations were introduced by my friend, Dr. Michael Allen, the Jockey Club's Medical Adviser.

All the time I served at Ayr Racecourse, the doctors, unlike the Vets, took no fees. But we were always given a sumptuous free lunch either in Western House with wives, or in the Owners and Trainers Lunch Room.

In my time, the late Earl of Eglinton, Chairman of the Club and a Senior Steward, always made sure that enough whisky was left in the Stewards Box to give the doctor a good tot at the end of the day's racing. Not being paid officials, we had somewhat more independence of action, which, paradoxically was an incentive to excel in the job.

Another advantage of not being paid a fee for a day at the Races was that one's 'fee' was 'in kind' and, therefore, not liable to be split either with the taxman or one's medical partners, as were other external appointments that carried a fee.

I was delighted to receive honorary life membership of the Western Meeting Club, and Aileen and I still very much enjoy a day's racing, with the odd flutter although neither of us are real experts on 'form'.

The Western Meeting Club, alas, is not now really a Club any longer in the true sense of the word. Through financial necessity, it had to open its doors wide to remain viable and it is now really a non-profit business. Ayr, however, is still one of the best tracks in the UK, with amenities as good as anywhere according to those who should know!

In the near future, The Western Meeting Club will give up its Club non-profit status and become a Limited Company. This should enable Ayr Racecourse to maintain its reputation as one of the premier Race Tracks in the country.

Children's Education

*N*ow, I must mention our children's education. Bruce, the eldest started at St. Margaret's, the local Catholic School in Ayr, and joined shortly afterwards by Tricia. Bruce then went to Carlekemp Priory School in North Berwick, a Benedictine Prep School that sent pupils on to either Fort Augustus School or Ampleforth as a rule. Sadly, Carlekemp and Fort Augustus School no longer exist as such. Tricia, and later, her two sisters, Susan and Amanda, had their education, in Hartfield, a very good little private school in Ayr, and the three of them eventually went to the Convent of the Holy Child Jesus in Harrogate.

After Speech Day – Carlekemp Preparatory School ~ 1957
Our young at North Berwick Harbour

Bruce went on to Ampleforth. It was very handy for us being able to see all four of them during half-terms and speech days etc., as Ampleforth and Harrogate were fairly near to each other. After Ampleforth, Bruce went to Trinity College, Dublin.

Bruce at Ampleforth
Early Sixties

Three Little Maids from School ~ 1958
Tricia, Susan and Amanda

Tricia, after school, went to Dundee University, Susan went to St. Andrews University and Amanda, like Bruce, went to Trinity, Dublin. They all managed to get Bachelor of Art Degrees. Bruce eventually became a Chartered Surveyor, Tricia a Teacher and Susan went to live in Australia after doing courses in Business Studies and such like. She has remained in Australia ever since, and luckily, we do see her from time to time. Amanda, after Trinity, was always very interested in the media and she had very good jobs both in radio and journalism until very sadly her life was cut short in May 1988.

Paradoxically, the sudden and huge rise of inflation in the Seventies following the global oil price crisis, when the price of oil went through the roof, was a disaster for those who had saved all their lives, or who were relatively wealthy. In our case, our overdraft was astronomical in relation to our earnings. At one point, our school fees exceeded our total annual income. But for us, inflation suddenly decimated our overdraft, whilst our income and eventually pensions, became linked to inflation.

My father-in-law's moral and financial support by setting up a Trust for the duration of our children's education, enabled us to pay enormous school fees which were, to a large extent, repaid as our overdraft was more or less cleared when the Trust matured. It is worth recalling that the Trustees, a firm of Brokers, refused to pay me the proceeds of the Trust on maturity, as they maintained that the proceeds were entirely for the children's welfare at the present time, not to pay me back for school fees which I had already paid myself. This was a bombshell, which coincided with my severe illness due to the Russian Bug. However, I went to London, saw the man in charge of the Trust, as my father-in-law had died by this time. He obviously reckoned that I was on my last legs and released the Trust money to me. I think that this must have aided my recovery!

Bruce at Fionnphort, Isle of Mull ~ 1965

Taken by Uncle Robert

180

Patricia

Susan

Amanda

Amanda ~ RIP May 1988
Laid to rest in Prestwick Cemetery

Travel after Retiral

*A*fter I retired from Medical Practice and Aileen from Dental Practice, Aileen and I, who both enjoyed worldwide travelling, visited many different countries. I will try not to be boring with a travelogue, but suffice to say we visited Hong Kong in 1979, just before my retirement. This was on a British Medical Association world trip. There, we were superbly entertained by Aileen's sister, Patricia and her top legal husband, Desmond Mayne. In 1981, the year I retired from the NHS, we did a round world trip, visiting USA, Hawaii, New Zealand, Australia, Hong Kong and India, where we revisited 'Firdaus' in Bombay and climbed to the roof where romance had first blossomed! We made many trips to Hong Kong where Bruce had emigrated in 1981 to work very successfully in the property business. Not only did we have wonderful hospitality from Bruce, but we also visited Sri Lanka, Japan, Vietnam and Thailand as his guests, later also being guests of his lovely wife, Nicky.

We saw Zimbabwe at a family wedding in 1992. Aileen's nephew married a lovely Zimbabwean lady, whose father is a British 'expat', her mother of several generations of Rhodesians.

One of our Hong Kong trips was to go by rail across the vast expanse of Russia, Mongolia and China – Moscow to Beijing on the Trans Siberian railway, and then through China by rail to Hong Kong. We also had a wonderful rail trip, as Bruce's guests, on the Orient Express from London to Venice in 1988.

A few years later, we crossed the USA by rail, east to west and back through Canada, including through the fabulous Rockies, all by rail. We visited several cousins both in Kentucky and

Vancouver Island – the Reids, and in Maine – the Nees, who were, as usual, extremely hospitable. We also visited cousin Hugh Walker in Toronto and his daughter, Zoë, in Toronto, and later, his other daughter Kim, in Boston.

Aileen and Percy – across USA & Canada by train ~ 1995

We had many trips to France, Germany, Austria, Italy and Spain, mainly by railway. We always preferred sightseeing to sun worshipping!

A recent memorable trip was to Spain by rail in 1999. we sailed from Portsmouth to Bilbao, then by train to Salamanca, Madrid, Seville, Granada and Cordova. We also visited cousins Ian and Mhairi Walker in Andalucía.

Our second daughter, Susan, settled in New South Wales in Australia, having married Paul Baldock, so we had a couple of great trips there, too. Aileen made one extra trip when, very sadly, poor Susan and Paul's third son, a baby, was a Cot Death victim in 1986. However, Alex and Jake are super boys, 19 and

17 as I write. Alex is a virtuoso piper, a Pipe Major when in Scots School Pipe Band at Bathurst. Jake, also a piper, is an outstanding athlete.

Alex is now at the University of Sydney.

Our elder daughter, Patricia married Ian Cowan. That has been, for all concerned, an ideal marriage, producing our first grandchild Rebecca, then Emma and Oliver, all of whom we are extremely proud. We make many forays south of the border visiting Cowans.

Susan with little Alex and Jacob
Little Bentfield, Wattleflat, NSW

Alex and Jacob Baldock – Pipers
Alex was Pipe Major of Scots School Band, Bathurst, NSW

Emma, Ian and Rebecca Cowan, with Poppy
Bentfield ~ Summer 1991

Amanda and Jessica ~ Christmas 1986
Bentfield

Granny Aileen with Jessica ~ 1985

Oliver Cowan ~ 1994

Jessica with Ken the cat ~ 1999

Emma is an outstanding 'Oars Person' – at present in the Thames Rowing Club First Ladies Eight, with hopes of international status.

As I have previously mentioned, we suffered a terrible sadness in 1988 losing our beautiful Amanda in a drowning accident in the Mediterranean. She was on holiday with her husband Matthew Bannister and their little daughter Jessica, then aged 3. This was a body blow, but we survived it with perpetual happy memories of this real character of a girl. Matthew remarried to a great friend of Amanda's and a grand little half-brother for Jessica was soon produced – Joseph – and this set-up is a great consolation. Jessica, now 17 in 2002, is a joy to us – so Amanda lives on!

Patricia now lives in Gloucestershire in a lovely house by the River Severn, and Susan lives in another lovely house, largely built by her husband, Paul in Wattleflat, New South Wales. Jessica is now in a very happy family in London, the Bannisters; Matthew being her father, Shelagh her stepmother and Joseph her half-brother.

The Bannister Family – Matthew, Shelagh, Jessica, Joseph
with Dillie Keane in the middle – at our Golden Wedding Party ~ June 1996

193

Aileen and Jessica – Camellias, Bentfield ~ 1998

Other Members of the Family

A note on other members of the family: Uncle Robert Reid, my mother's only brother, emigrated first to Canada and then to the USA after the First World War. He, like his fellow gunners on the Irvine Battery Royal Artillery, had had a very rough time and was in poor health, which made him decide to leave his native Ayrshire. Also, the family home, East Balgray, near Irvine, a lovely farm with house attached, had been let to a tenant farmer, a Mr. Young, who let the place go to rack and ruin – it is not much better now, sadly. My grandfather could not get Young evicted. This was a sad ending for the home of the Reids for many generations.

East Balgray - Percy, Hilary and Robert ~ 1998
Home of Robert Reid and his forebears near Irvine

195

Uncle Robert came home frequently, being a fanatical traveller and photographer. He gave young Bruce and his cousin, Robin Gardiner, second son of Mary Breckenridge, wonderful holidays in California during their school holidays.

My father-in-law, J.P. Digby, died on 24 February 1968, just a day after his 50th Wedding Anniversary. Sadly for him, the business that he built up, *Pye Ireland*, which was a great success manufacturing and marketing radio and television sets, was fatally crippled when the Duty on British products sold in the Irish Republic was abolished.

His elder son, Aileen's brother Dillon, had qualified as a Doctor but J.P. Digby, keen to have the business successor in the family, gave Dillon the job of looking after the firm. Dillon presided over the demise of Pye Ireland through no fault of his own. He was, however, too decent a chap to be wide-awake to the infighting of the business world.

Myles, the youngest of the family was just the opposite of Dillon. He knew everyone around, and was as alert to peoples' scheming ways as Dillon was unaware. Myles had the same quick mind as his father, but sadly, for himself mainly, he could never take life and work too seriously. A combination of the two brothers brains in one head would have been a great success story.

Patricia, the second-born Digby offspring, Aileen being first, qualified as an Architect and she was exceptionally good. She had done wonderful work in East Africa and, subsequently, Hong Kong, where she still resides as I write in 2002. She married Desmond Mayne, a Barrister, who had a brilliant career in Hong Kong until his untimely death a few years ago.

My mother-in-law, Mrs. Jean Digby, came from a long established family of landowners, with the family name of Laine, in the West of Ireland. This family suffered under the Land Reform Acts and Aileen's grandfather died some years after a hunting accident. His wife, Aileen's Granny, was a really wonderful lady. Sadly, I never met her, but she held her head up high, rearing a large family – one son and five daughters.

Jane Laine, née Dillon, Aileen's maternal Grandmother

Jean, the second youngest of the Laine girls, married J.P. Digby, as I have said. Her small stature belied her amazing personality. In later years, she spent quite a lot of time as a widow with us in *Bentfield*. I recall evenings in our sun room, listening to records of Count John McCormack, when with a wee dram, which we would call an 'eclipse', she would say "All this and heaven too!"

Kathleen, my sister, the eldest of the family, did great work in the VADs in wartime. Her main job after the war was as a Matron in Schools, which was a job in which she excelled. She was not an academic, but was wonderful with people. She absolutely loved all her nieces and nephews who all loved her, too.

Kathleen in her new home in Loans, Troon
just across the road from Rowantree Cottage ~ 1990

My brother, Robert, after the war, continued working with the *Saxone Shoe Company*, footwear manufacturers in Kilmarnock. The Managing Director of the firm, Jack Abbot, a brother of my cousin Alex Walker's wife Sunny Abbot, was very impressed with Robert as a youngster. Robert repeatedly telephoned Mr. Abbot about canaries and fox terriers about which Jack Abbot was an expert. He said to my father once, "Tom, if you ever want to find that boy a job, let me know." Robert worked his way up in the shoe trade and was eventually Deputy Managing Director of the *British Shoe Corporation* when he retired. His great forte, apart from his business skills, was getting on with, and knowing his workforce, like my father before him. He married Hilary Smith of Troon in 1955, and has two boys and a girl, all happily married with families.

Campbell, 13 years younger than myself, was not surprisingly, very affected by my father, his namesake's death, when he was a young schoolboy. However, he has made a great success of his life in various firms connected mainly with electronics. He is a super DIY man with a very inventive mind. He married Patricia McConnell of Harrogate and has two boys and a girl and several grandchildren.

I could relate more histories of my many cousins and relations, but I shall let them write their own autobiographies!

Three Walker Brothers with their wives ~ July 1995
at West Callipers

Percy & Aileen, Robert & Hilary, Campbell & Pat, Kathleen and Myles,
Dillon & June
At the time of our 40th Wedding Anniversary

Improving Bentfield

*S*ince the beginning of our time in *Bentfield*, where we moved in the summer of *1954,* we gradually improved the house both inside and outside and in the garden.

Our first ploy in the late fifties was to build garden walls mainly for shelter. *Bentfield*, although a moderately large house with six bedrooms and two bathrooms when we first moved in, lacked any outside buildings, i.e. garage, sheds or even a place to keep coal and wood for the fires. So, luckily we spotted very old cottages being demolished in Whitletts, formerly a village just outside Ayr, but now well within the town limits. These cottages were stone-built, but were condemned for human habitation. So we persuaded the demolition contractors to dump the old stones in our garden, which was very convenient for them as well. We discovered a really good stonemason, Angus Swanson, who built high walls near the house that, as well as being windbreaks, created a yard near the house where we built a garden shed, tool shed and greenhouse.

The alignment of the new wall on the seaward, or western side, of the house was built exactly in line with the front, i.e. west side, of the house, and had an arched gate leading to the front lawn. The garden, so called, consisted entirely of sand dunes, and it really looked as if we were wildly optimistic in expecting anything to grow except for the indigenous bents grasses. The only living thing in the whole garden was a solitary, half dead, laburnum tree. But, we were determined to make a garden, with both of us very keen on gardens in our youth; especially Aileen who often thought that horticulture was a better career than dentistry! As I have already said, we now have a forest and a garden!

Bentfield in the 1950s

Tennis Court before trees

Sea frontage before sunroom and new bedroom

I consider our fitness, despite our age in 2002, to be ascribed to the hard but joyful work in the garden over the years.

In 1974, we decided to build a sunroom or conservatory facing the sea. The existing house and the new wall created the perfect setting for this enormously successful addition to the house. The view from it is ever changing in all weathers, but the sunsets are the icing on the cake. In the eighties, we decided to demolish a rather crudely built bedroom and bathroom on the southern aspect, which in the thirties or forties had been grafted onto the house by Mr. Hector McArthur. Up until then this had been Tricia's bedroom, she seemed to love the isolation of it. So we rebuilt the bedroom and bathroom, which made a huge difference to the amenities of the house, especially for guests.

The Shortest Day ~ View from Bentfield

Sunset between Mainland and Ailsa Craig ~ on the longest day, we see sunset over the south end of Bute

Bentfield showing Sun Room ~ Summer 1997
before extending south extension in 2000

In 1989, we decided to enlarge the kitchen. Originally, it had a very old kitchen range, coal fired, which was extremely labour intensive and a coal guzzler. We replaced it with an electric cooker, but the kitchen was always an irritation, being impossible to put cupboards, sinks and fittings in the optimum places, in spite of it being a fairly large room. So we embarked on a major project. We knocked a hole in the 3ft outer wall into the existing yard where there had been a wooden garage previously. This open space was supported by temporary props. The builder said, "It is safe, unless we have an earthquake!" A seismic shock was recorded that very night in Edinburgh, the night of the San Francisco earthquake!

We thus created a lovely eating area adjacent to the greatly improved kitchen, now being able to put all cupboards, sinks, fridges and freezers etc., in the most convenient places. We also installed an *Aga* Cooker, all-electric, as we have no oil or gas supply. This project has been hugely successful, and we eat all meals in the eating area except on special occasions when the dining room springs to life!

New kitchen extension – completed 1990

Project New Guest Wing ~ 2000

Our final major project was in the year 2000 – to extend the guest bedroom. Built in the eighties, we knocked down part of the wall of the bedroom on the southern aspect and built on a bathroom complex with all modern facilities, including a shower. We also greatly increased space for built-in wardrobes and drawers. This has been a tremendous success, not only for guests, but we expect many years ahead that going up and down stairs to our existing bedroom may be difficult. At present it is very good exercise.

As I write, we can say that we have achieved all our desires as far as making *Bentfield* a wonderful home for our family and ourselves, and it is a great joy to invite our friends to share our happiness.

We are so incredibly lucky to have in our cottage a lovely couple who could not do more for us, being as helpful as they are and also remaining cheerful. I think one of my favourite noises nowadays is laughter in the kitchen – Aileen and Lorraine Hayes sharing a joke!

John and Lorraine Hayes who live in our Cottage,
with Aileen ~ 2001

206

Some Main Events at *Bentfield*

*I*t was always a great joy to us to entertain our friends at *Bentfield* especially to hear them say, "What a view," and to admire our efforts at aforestation and horticulture in such a hostile environment, due to wind and salt spray off the sea.

Our children often filled the available floor space with their friends in sleeping bags when all the beds were full.

We were always so encouraged and delighted when our elderly aunts, uncles and in-laws visited.

I sometimes now sit in the Drawing Room, reminiscing about the many friends and relations who have shared our home at many parties and visits. With a glass of malt in my hand, I can sometimes hear their voices from the past!

Several occasions stand out above the others. The wedding of our eldest daughter, Patricia, when she married Ian Cowan in August 1973. This was a spectacular event, not least due to the marquee blowing down on the eve of the wedding! But it was a lovely day and as Jane Digby, Aileen's niece remarked, all pulling guy ropes together, while tent pegs were being hammered in again, was a great bonding process for the guests!

1976 ~ Tricia and Ian and tiny Rebecca had come up from their home in Barnard Castle, Co. Durham, laden with delicious food and drink. All was prepared at Rowantree Cottage without us having the slightest inkling of what was afoot. This was a 'This is Your Life!' surprise for Aileen and myself. We were totally ignorant of the ploy until we arrived back from a drinks party at the Dicksons of Symington, where we were kept, for a reason we knew not, until the 'all clear' was given – and so a spectacular party took place on the lawn at *Bentfield* on our Thirtieth Wedding Anniversary

Tricia's Wedding ~ 3 August 1973
Our Lady and St Meddan Church, Troon

1986 ~ 40 glorious years! Another large drinks party on the lawn at *Bentfield* in gorgeous weather.

1996 ~ 50 glorious years! A beautiful marquee on the lawn, groaning with food and drink and a guest list of relations and friends from far and near. Bruce's surprise was T-shirts with US TWO in 1946 on the back and 1996 on the front, issued to all lunchtime guests on the Sunday morning following. He also had a video digest on screen with the highlights of our Fifty Years.

Tricia followed up these gatherings at the lovely Cowan home on the banks of the *Severn* with lavish family parties for all ages celebrating Aileen in 1999 and me in 2001, all of us being of a certain age, in my case 85.

The 1996 party and subsequent ones at *The Priory*, the Cowan's house, are all recorded on video.

We have had other parties on the lawn, entertaining golfing societies from overseas and we always seem to have been blessed with glorious weather.

Our 50ᵗʰ Wedding Anniversary celebrations, Bentfield ~ June 1996

*Percy, Fergus, Tricia, Bruce, Susan and Aileen ~ Golden Anniversary
with T-shirts ~ 1996*

The Priory – Tricia, Becca, Oliver, Emma and Aileen ~ 1999

The Priory – Aileen's Feast ~ August 1999
The day after AWRE

The Priory – Percy's Feast ~ 8 July 2001
Cowans, Walkers, Digbys, Stingemores, Cartys, Normans and Dillie
Keane

211

Family Weddings

*B*efore leaving the subject of parties and weddings, I must mention Susan marrying Paul Baldock in Australia in 1981. Aileen, Bruce and I went to New South Wales at Susan's request to approve of Paul, which we certainly did. We had a terrific party and wedding celebration in their lovely house and garden in Wattleflat, New South Wales. The five of us all went on their honeymoon together, visiting innumerable Aussie Walker relations, most of whom had replicated the Walker Christian names. We still have a steady flow of Australian cousins visiting us.

Susan and Paul's Wedding, Little Bentfield ~ 1981
Wattleflat, NSW

Amanda's wedding to Matthew Bannister in 1985 took place in London at Amanda's request, as she had so many friends in London and had lived most of the time there since leaving University. It was a lovely occasion in Stoke Newington Parish Church, with the ceremony being conducted by the Rev. Roger Royle, the very well known radio Parson. A great reception in Hampstead followed in beautiful surroundings. The occasion was marked by the presence of many Irish and Scottish relations, in addition to Amanda's and Matthew's numerous London friends.

Amanda and Matthew's wedding ~ 1984
Stoke Newington Parish Church, London

In 1991, having proposed to Nicky on a holiday on an off-shore China Island, (we visited the hallowed spot with them a year later) Bruce made arrangements to get married in the same church as Nicky's parents had been married – Checkendon Church in Oxfordshire. Michael and Phillipa Hall, Nicky's parents, must have been staggered by the number of guests whom Bruce and Nicky mustered, together with masses of Irish and Scottish relations, as well as their own friends. The most lavish reception and later, dancing, in a magnificent country house hotel Danesfield on the Thames between Marlow and Henley ensued.

Luckily, this occasion was also immortalised on a video.

Aileen and I joined the newlyweds for lunch where they had spent their wedding night – *Cliveden* – the ultimate in opulence.

The happy couple honeymooned in Botswana and Namibia before returning to their home in Shek O, Hong Kong, where in due course, Digby, Roland and Magnus arrived to join them.

Bruce and Nicky pledging their troth ~ 1990
Gulang Yu, off China

Bruce and Nicky's wedding ~ 1991
Danesfield House, Oxfordshire

Ponies and Pets

I now come to an important part of our lives – Ponies and Pets. When our children's ages varied from Bruce about 12 to Amanda about 6, we always had at least one pony at *Bentfield*. Before the garden became a garden, we had the ponies grazing in a fenced off field and when we went on holiday we could always find a friendly farmer to take them in.

Our first pony was a piebald old timer called '*Paint*'. He had been part of the family both of Tullochs of Lockerbie and Walkers of Newark. He would let our kids do anything, such as having three up at once, and he was really too old to be of any risk to them. Next, we had a younger, more sprightly and smaller piebald, '*Tiddlywinks*'.

All four children adored the ponies and were very active in the Eglinton Pony Club, attending Rallies and Hunt Meets regularly.

We acquired a lovely grey mare, *Rosie*, who although slow and placid was a wonderful jumper. Our kids sometimes lost marks when *Rosie* would stop at a jump or fence and leap over the obstacle from a standing start. Just before we parted with *Rosie*, she gave birth to a foal. We called her *Freesia* because she had the same colour scheme as Friesian Cattle. Tommy Goldie's *Sikander* was the stallion.

Pony people are always only too willing to share their ponies with other pony people, especially when their children had outgrown them, so we often had visiting ponies on long-term loan, *Sparky*, another grey, *Dora* and *Jura*, which meant that all four children could be mounted for the same event

Tiddlywinks, Tricia, Susan, Amanda and Saki ~ Bentfield 1958

Tiddlywinks hungry – Bentfield
Aileen, Susan, Tricia and Amanda – Saki and Topper watch

Rosie and foal, Freesia ~ Bentfield, Easter 1966

Jura, Sparky and Rosie ~ Easter 1967

Patricia grooming Rosie, with Susan in shorts
preparing for Craigie Show

Our four Equestrians ~ about 1963

Pony Club Camps were forever the highlight of the children's summer holidays. We were always on good terms with the local contractors and farmers who would box our ponies to and from events. It was all great fun, especially the frantic times getting the ponies ready, grooming, oiling hooves, tail bandages and cleaning tack. Not unnaturally, mother, Aileen, had to be on top of everything to make sure that our ponies and riders were in immaculate order – hard work!

Tricia and Susan kept up the pony tradition with their families, Tricia being involved with her new Pony Club and her children Rebecca and Emma were as keen as their mother before them.

Rebecca and Emma with their ponies Skipper and Magic
The Priory ~ Christmas 1991

Amanda graduated from ponies to hunters. For a while, we kept a mare, *Yellow Gorse* that belonged to Keith Tulloch, and Amanda regularly hunted with the Eglinton Hunt. She, later, whilst working in London, took on the awesome job of exercising polo ponies. One exercise was to ride full tilt at a wall, turning at the last possible moment – essential training for fast movement on the polo field.

The pony ethic was a wonderful holiday occupation. Our children made many life-long friends many of whom were also schoolmates. It was a very healthy life style for them; there were no computer games then! Luckily, we have endless reminders of those happy days on video. I had all of the several miles of our ciné films since 1929 converted to video. To view these records on tape would make a good illustrated guide for the reader of these memoirs!

I must also refer to other livestock in our lives. We were all great animal lovers, so we were never without a dog. *Topper*, was a wire-haired Fox Terrier, third of his line, and was around in the children's very early days. He loved sitting with the patients in the Waiting Room at the New Road Surgery. All dog owners think that their dog is the best in the world, so I shall not enlarge on this theme, although it was true in our case! G.K. Chesterton once said something like this: "If entry to Heaven was based upon merit rather than favour, dogs would be far more likely to enter Heaven than their human masters."

Next we had *Kaffy*, a Cairn terrier of very independent mind, who never missed a day of being absent without leave!

We walked two Beagles from the Ampleforth College pack whilst Bruce was at school there. It broke our hearts and theirs when we had to return them to the pack.

In spite of Aileen being strongly allergic to cat fur; we had a string of lovely Siamese cats – starting with *Saki*, whose nights were spent under each child's sheet in strict rotation. Then *Oedipuss*, and his mate, *Anonypuss*, who turned up from still we know not where. Once we advertised that *Oedipuss* was missing, but he returned on his own, emaciated after three weeks on the run, and lived happily thereafter with his mate. *Jason* was our last Siamese, and he shared his life with *Rosebud*, a fluffy wee Persian whom Susan had rescued from the 'chop' whilst at St. Andrews.

When *Kaffy*, an incredible survivor in spite of his wanderings, eventually went through the Heavyside Layer, we branched out on Black Labradors. Tricia already had a lovely black Lab, *Cleo*, who produced a very special son, *Fingal*. Although not 100% pure bred, he was of extraordinary intelligence. Like his master, he golfed every Thursday at Prestwick, where he is still a legend.

When the sad time came for *Fingal's* departure, we were dogless for a short while. It was too painful for us, so a friend produced a Border terrier (who was crossed with a first cousin Lakeland terrier.) *Fergus*, now 10, has more personality than I can describe. He still lives with us, very sprightly, with his dear friend black Lab, *Fingal II*, who is a most loving and loveable chap, but, being a very pure bred handsome chap, somewhat lacks the almost human characteristics of his predecessor, *Fingal I*.

Fingal II and Fergus

Apart from hens, budgies and mice, that is about all I can relate about pets between 1946 and 2002.

Random thoughts about the Present Day

Before concluding this saga, I must record a few random thoughts about the present day.

The physical health of the nation is probably better than it has ever been. The shortcomings of the National Health Service are never out of the news, but people tend to forget what it was like pre-NHS. We moan about the length of waiting lists – pre-NHS there was little to wait for! The downside is the fact that so many people seem to be suffering from 'stress', the 'in' word. Life seems to be a rat race. Money has taken first place in peoples ambitions, so our values of what gives rise to happiness and contentment are being replaced by self-interest. Whereas religion used to be the guiding light in our lives, the majority, sadly, of our countrymen seem to have become estranged from the simple ethic of Christianity. I am sure that our Nation still thirsts for the 'peace that the world cannot give', but they do not seek the answer. It is not entirely surprising that many aspects of the Church seem to 'switch off' our young, but it seems that a more enlightened attitude in the churches may, hopefully, reverse the trend of empty churches.

It's a pity that John Major's exhortation "Back to Basics" was so ridiculed.

Pollution: Pollution of the land and the atmosphere is also a terrifying problem. Toxic wastes in the sea, the air and on land are already having disastrous effect on the animal kingdom, destroying nature's food chain that has been evolved over uncountable centuries. I even heard recently that oestrogen levels in our rivers and in the sea are making male fish sterile and that, in time, we human fish eaters may suffer the same fate – what a thought!

Slaughter of our Forests: We are denuding huge tracts of ancient forests. Soon, what were once forests will be like the Sahara Desert – and what will replace timber?

Global warming: This is already causing the Arctic and Antarctic ice to melt at a alarming rate, caused by pollution of the atmosphere, the consequences of which are accelerating to an extent that even our grandchildren may be affected by rising water levels flooding low lying land.

Drugs: This is probably the worst problem of all. Drug pushers and drug barons make fortunes out of the utter misery and degradation, often deaths, of those who fall into the temptation of using and experimenting with drugs. The problem is escalating. It will get a lot worse before our young ones are sufficiently convinced or brave enough to say 'NO'.

Terrorism: There have been instances of terrorists, so called, graduating to Freedom Fighters and then on to becoming Statesmen, for example General Smuts of South Africa and Boer War fame. But today's terrorists are utterly callous, evil and perverted in a totally unjustifiable way in their understandable desperation to achieve their aims. It is therefore perfectly understandable that, horrific acts of terrorism, for example the Twin Towers of 11 September 2001, should be followed by the most energetic attempts to bring the culprits to justice. But, it is also only too true that fighting terrorists produces more terrorists in an unending succession, which defeats its own object. History will always reveal the injustices that have given rise to terrorism. It is to try to rectify these injustices that we must strive towards. If we do not, then there will be no end to mankind's hatred and suspicion and killing of each other.

I wonder whether the possession of nuclear weapons, which are undoubtedly weapons of mass destruction, would in fact make even the most evil aggressor stop and think before unleashing such weapons on an enemy. Would the Soviet Union have used them against their perceived enemies if these enemies themselves were not also nuclear powers?

One Line on Celebrities: Overpaid, over-sexed and over-exposed. What role models are these for the young of our Country?

Racism: It is inevitable, and it should be a good thing that Britain should accept people from all over the world, especially from our former Empire, as equal citizens. But the world is in such a mess that many very undesirable anarchists, whose bosses are bent on Revolution of the World Order, have infiltrated our society. Furthermore, so many immigrants perceive themselves, often with justification, as Second Class Citizens. Many are unemployed, although some, being very clever and hard working have over-taken the indigent whites, both on income and living standards. On the whole, the Asian immigrants have done better for them-selves than the Afro-Caribbean stock. This alone, causes intense jealousy between the two black cultures.

The Asian young, having seen the culture of their grandparents and parents being superseded by the typically *laissez faire* attitude of the host country, have sadly lost the sense of discipline and responsibility of the strict religious creed of their forebears. So, in the inner cities, especially with nothing else to do, Whites indulge in 'Paki bashing'. Pakistanis and Bangladeshis indulge in 'White and Afro bashing' and the three races are being polarised. Very sad.

Devolution ~ i.e. Home Rule for Scotland

I welcomed the concept of a Scottish Parliament whole-heartedly. Since its inception in 1999, this completely new body has done some excellent things, dealing with the problems that would have been neglected by Westminster. It still has a lot to learn.

However, I am passionately in favour of Scotland remaining part of the United Kingdom.

Our beloved Queen Elizabeth (second of England, first of Scotland) is sometimes referred to as "The Queen of England" – this hurts! The British Monarch, in the person of our Queen, is also Head of the Commonwealth of Nations, most, if not all of whom, were either Dominions or Colonies of the British Empire in former times. Nearly all of these Commonwealth countries are autonomous states, some even Republics.

But our Queen, due to her dedication, affection and personality, has kept the concept of Commonwealth alive in a manner that no mere political Head of State could. Let us hope that world leaders in the rich countries can contrive to rid the less fortunate poorer countries of their crippling debts.

The Monarchy stands above partisan politics and is the most powerful symbol of the unity of our Country, regardless of the fact that political power has to a large extent been devolved to the component parts of the British Nation.

The English and Scots really do get on well together and I am no Scottish Nationalist. I do, however, get irritated by some English perceptions. The English tend to say 'England' when they really mean 'Britain', but when they say 'Scotland', or when a Scot says 'Scotland', for that matter, it is not Britain they mean. The English media confuse me at times. Sometimes, the 'North' means the 'North of England' and, sometimes, especially with weather forecasters, 'The North' includes Scotland. I have given up worrying when radio and TV garden presenters tell me: "Oh that would never grow in Scotland." The West of Scotland has milder winters than East Anglia. Our rainfall, like our accents, is as variable geographically as is the case in England.

The Football Association, The Rugby Union, (even The Royal Navy) have no prefix, unlike Scotland, Ireland, Wales and other countries. Why?

I do admit, however, that the word 'England' has a more poetic ring to it than the word 'Britain', and I can understand Parry preferring 'England's green and pleasant land' in his 'Jerusalem'.

Very sadly, it seems that our new Parliament is already riding rough shod over the sizeable minority of our country. I think it is true that 20% of the population of Scotland occupy 80% of the land. But the Parliament consists of at least 80% of members who have exclusively an urban background. So, in spite of far more pressing matters, they have spent a large of amount of time and effort in banning Hunting Mammals with Dogs. So, the ancient sport of Fox Hunting, still the most humane way of culling foxes is to be banned. It seems that our urban masters find chasing and terrifying cuddly little foxes too cruel for a civilised country. I suspect that if foxes were to be hunted by hunters on foot, not dressed up as 'Toffs' in Pink Coats on horseback, the foxes' welfare would be totally disregarded by our urban Parliamentarians.

Now, another great problem – New Land Reform ideas abound that apparently will give tenants the right to buy their landlord's land on which they live as tenants. Whilst this might redress the balance of rapacious absentee landlords of the past *vis á vis* their impoverished tenants, this just does not happen in Scotland today. Management of land and rivers nowadays is very big business, especially for our chief source of income – Tourism.

If the land is to be managed piecemeal by innumerable small-holders, will they have the know-how or the wherewithal to maintain their newly acquired bounty? Even worse, what safe-guards will there be to prevent former tenants selling their newly acquired property to 'Developers' at an enormous profit? It all sounds like a battle between the 'haves' and the 'have-nots'. This is sad when the new Scottish Parliament envisaged by the great man, the late Donald Dewar, was to be offering fair deals for all.

Bruce's Homecoming

Bruce and Nicky ~ Hong Kong 1995
On the occasion the Royal Hong Kong Regiment Disbandment Ball
at Government House

*I*n June 2000, Bruce and Nicky, with Digby, Roland and Magnus decided to leave Hong Kong for Scotland. They had had their eye on the most beautiful old property, Knock Castle, just north of Largs, Ayrshire, for several years. They had the first option to buy when the then owner, General Sir Richard Lawson, decided to leave. So, when the house came on the market, they had to act quickly, which they did. It had been Bruce's intention to sail home from Hong Kong to the UK in his large Catamaran that he had purchased mainly with that end in view. Aileen and I had mixed feelings about the advisability of such a trip. Nicky, being very sporting in every sense of the word, persuaded herself to be keen on the project, but the problem was soon solved by Knock suddenly coming on the market. But, instead of jumping on an aeroplane which they had done many times before, they decided to come home entirely by land and sea, strictly without using other than public transport and no taxis!

22 The Headland, Shek O, Hong Kong
The balcony overlooking South China Sea

229

So, one day, they left their lovely home in Shek O, Hong Kong Island, overlooking the South China Sea. They were piped out of Shek O Village, boarded the No.9 China bus, onto the Mass Transit Underground Railway to Kowloon Railway Station, where they entrained for Beijing in a new state-of-the-art train. Sightseeing in Beijing included the Great Wall of China, then the Trans-Siberian Railway to Moscow – more sightseeing there and on by rail to St. Petersburg, yet more sightseeing there and on by rail again to Tallin in Estonia. Still more sightseeing and across the Baltic to Stockholm, and then on to Gothenburg by train. Next, they sailed across the North Sea from Gothenburg to Newcastle on Tyne, and then another train, The Sprinter from Newcastle to Ayr direct.

Ayr Station ~ 30 June 2000
Hong Kong to Scotland overland!

We met the travellers at Ayr Station, all in wonderful fettle having thoroughly enjoyed the experience. The Sprinter did not stop at Prestwick, so Aileen and the travellers entrained back to Prestwick from Ayr where they were met by a crowd of old mates and a welcoming Piper! I took the baggage on to Prestwick in our car,

whilst the family all walked from Prestwick Station to *Bentfield -
Home* on 30 June 2000. It was an epic trip!

Knock Castle, Largs
Bruce and Nicky moved in July 2000

Three Men in a tub, with Granny Aileen
Bentfield ~ 2000

231

It is great to have at least some of our family nearby, especially watching the wee boys grow up and seeing and hearing all about their many and varied experiences. Largs is a wonderful place for sporting activities having the Inverclyde Sports Centre and access to adjacent Islands such as Cumbrae, Bute and Arran.

Nicky is an expert skier, especially in Cross-Country, as this is her No.1 sport. She and the boys are also very competent downhill skiers, including Bruce!

Bruce and Nicky with their three boys ~ 6 May 2001
Digby's Confirmation and first Communion, Largs

So, as I write this in January 2002, I never forget how lucky we both are to be healthy and young at heart (and also in body for our ages).

We have a lovely family, lovely friends and a lovely house and garden in a lovely country.

Who could ask for anything more!

Aileen and Percy ~ Bentfield, Summer 1999

*on the garden seat made from a Thai horse-drawn cart – a present
from Bruce and Nicky on our 50th wedding Anniversary ~ 1996*

Aileen and Percy ~ Bentfield 2000